TWAYNE'S WORLD AUTHORS SERIES

A Survey of the World's Literature

Sylvia E. Bowman, Indiana University

GENERAL EDITOR

NETHERLANDS

Egbert Krispyn, University of Florida

EDITOR

Jean LeClerc

(TWAS 209)

TWAYNE'S WORLD AUTHORS SERIES (TWAS)

The purpose of TWAS is to survey the major writers
—novelists, dramatists, historians, poets, philosophers,
and critics—of the nations of the world. Among the
national literatures covered are those of Australia,
Canada, China, Eastern Europe, France, Germany,
Greece, India, Italy, Japan, Latin America, the Netherlands, New Zealand, Poland, Russia, Scandinavia, Spain,
and the African nations, as well as Hebrew, Yiddish,
and Latin Classical literatures. This survey is comple-
mented by Twayne's United States Authors Series
and English Authors Series.

The intent of each volume in these series is to present
a critical-analytical study of the works of the writer;
to include biographical and historical material that
may be necessary for understanding, appreciation,
and critical appraisal of the writer and to present all
material in clear, concise English—but not to vitiate
the scholarly content of the work by doing so.

Jean LeClerc

By SAMUEL A. GOLDEN
Wayne State University

Twayne Publishers, Inc.   ::   New York

To Elisabeth

Preface

The general aims of this study of Jean LeClerc are to show his effectiveness as an intermediary in Anglo-Dutch intellectual crosscurrents during the late seventeenth and early eighteenth centuries and to expand knowledge of the intricacies involved in the formation and movement of ideas basic to a fuller understanding of the so-called Age of Reason.

LeClerc's amazingly voluminous output imposes the hard and often arbitrary task of proper selection from his writings to reach a fair evaluation of his worth, but limitation does not mean presentation of only a partial view. LeClerc is often repetitious and at times encumbers his thought with needless and distracting details. This condition is, it seems, inevitable because it arises chiefly from total dedication to the single belief that truth can be reached by the proper use of reason.

This evaluation centers about LeClerc's three *Bibliothèques,* which are a remarkable repository not only of reviews of books of contemporary interest but also of commentary and citation of the writings and ideas of the greatest minds of his age. In addition, there is presented description and brief analysis of some of his other writings to offer an extended and clearer view of his own thought.

Since LeClerc's writings are still widely scattered, this study owes much to the cooperation received from the staffs at the British Museum, the Universiteits Bibliotheek in Amsterdam and the Koninklijke Bibliotheek in The Hague. A Folger Shakespeare Library Fellowship and a Faculty Research Award from Wayne State University permitted me to conduct research under ideal conditions. I am pleased to express my thanks to both sources of encouragement.

SAMUEL A. GOLDEN

Wayne State University

Contents

Chronology

1657   Born in Geneva.
1683   After visiting London, settles in Amsterdam.
1684   Begins his career among the Remonstrants in Amsterdam under the aegis of Philip van Limborch.
1685   Writes *Sentimens de Quelques Théologiens de Hollande*. Meets John Locke.
1686   Begins *Bibliothèque Universelle et Historique*. Meets Gilbert Burnet.
1690   Revises Moreri's *Dictionnaire Historique*.
1691   Stops work on *Bibliothèque Universelle et Historique*. Marries Mary Leti. Plans to move to England.
1693-   Concentrates on biblical studies.
1695
1696   Brings out *Ars Critica* and *The Causes of Incredulity*.
1699   Brings out *Parrhasiana*, Part I. Meets Shaftesbury.
1700   Brings out *Parrhasiana*, Part II.
1703   Begins *Bibliothèque Choisie*.
1703-   Edits works of Erasmus.
1706
1707-   The Gabillon Imposture.
1708
1709   Brings out edition of Grotius's *The Truth of the Christian Religion*.
1712   Appointed Professor of Ecclesiastical History.
1713   Ends *Bibliothèque Choisie*.
1714   Begins *Bibliothèque Ancienne et Moderne*.
1727   Ends *Bibliothèque Ancienne et Moderne*.
1731   Brings out translation and commentary on Old Testament.
1736   Dies in Amsterdam.

CHAPTER 1

The Background

"Th' *increasing* Prospect *tires* our wandring Eyes,
Hills peep o'er Hills, and *Alps* on *Alps* arise!"

AS far back as medieval days Anglo-Dutch cultural and commercial ties were so well developed that in spite of hostility, ill-will, chauvinism, and prejudice, these bonds were occasionally frayed but never broken. While politicians, statesmen, princes, and warriors in both lands maintained their spectacular rivalries, scholars generally ignored them as they worked steadily to infuse fresh vigor into the life of the republic of letters. By the late seventeenth and early eighteenth centuries, cultural interests bound England and Holland.

Traditionally, the British had little sympathy for foreigners and the Dutch were no exception. English literature is full of supporting evidence. From Dekker and Webster's *Northward Hoe* (1607) to Dryden's *Amboyna* (1673) to Pope's *The Dunciad* (1743), British writers have left a long trail of prejudice and distrust. Walter Scott, in commenting on *Amboyna,* took an accurate measure of his countrymen when he wrote, "It is a characteristic of the English nation, that their habitual dislike against their neighbors is soon and easily blown into animosity." Of Dryden's attack on the Dutch, Scott noted, "The character of the Hollanders, as there represented, is too grossly vicious and detestable to give the least pleasure. They are neither men, nor even devils; but a sort of lubber fiends, compounded of cruelty, avarice, and brutal debauchery, like Dutch swabbers possessed by demons."[1]

Contemporary British attitudes toward the Dutch at the turn of the seventeenth century varied from that of John Tutchin to that of Daniel De Foe. Tutchin, after traveling "from *Leivarden* in *Friezland,* thro' *Holland*" characterized the people and their country as

A Land much differing from all other Soils,
Forc'd from the Sea, and buttress'd up with Piles.
No marble Quarrys bind the springy Ground,
But Loads of Sand and Cockle-shells are found:
Its Natives void of Honesty and Grace
A Boorish, rude, and an inhumane Race;
From Nature's Excrement their Life is drawn
Are born in Bogs, and nourish'd up from Spawn.[2]

At the other extreme, De Foe found that his true-born Englishman had Dutch blood in his veins. He wrote, "But when I see
the town full of lampoons and invectives against Dutchmen, only
because they are foreigners, . . . I confess myself moved by it
to remind our nation of their own original."[3]

No matter what the attitude, the British maintained keen
interest in the Dutch as may be noted in many pamphlets
describing their way of life, their government, and their country
in general. One typical example is *The Dutch Drawn to the Life*,
printed in 1664. The anonymous author advised the reader that
the Low Countries presented "a short Map and View of what the
whole World sheweth you at large" and that "there is not that
thing a Man or Nation need to Learn, that they [the Dutch]
cannot Teach." He listed among the great men of learning
"Erasmus, Lipsius, the two great Scalligers [*sic*] . . . the Douzas,
. . . Vossius, Grotius; Natives of this Country, [who] have been
the great Restorers of it [learning] to the World." He said their
religion was practical, countenancing only "Calvanisme, but for
Trade's sake they *Tolerate* all others, except the Papists . . . [and
that] there is full Liberty of Conscience: you may be what Devil
you will there, so you be but peaceable." He said Holland was a
place where "God may be more safely offended . . . than the
States General" and where "They allow all Opinions at home."
He described the Dutch language as a "Tongue as large as Europe, spoken in *Germany, Denmarke, Norway, Sweden,* and *England;* (for most of our old words are *Dutch,*) and so little altered
that it is in a manner the same as it was 2000. years ago, without
the too much mingled borrowings of their Neighbour Nations."[4]

Another pamphlet emphasized the strong Dutch interest in
learning. In *The Present State of the United Provinces of the
Low Countries. . .*, printed in 1669, an anonymous Englishman
described Leyden as a university having "alwayes . . . very famous
professors in all faculties. . . . The great Scaliger, and the incom-

parable Salmazius [*sic*] have been as the two great Lights ...
of this learn'd Firmament"; professors were "chosen with care,
and well recompenc'd [*sic*] for their labours." He praised the
Dutch for their libraries, private and public; he approved of
their liberty where "All that is reasonable, is lawfull." *"O happy*
Holland," he soliloquized, *"that hast preserv'd that precious jewel
of Liberty; preserve it well, for with its loss, goes that of thy
happiness!"* He pointed out that differences of religion were
tolerated even to the extent of accommodating Gomarists (the
Counter-Remonstrants) and Arminians, who "have never been
at quiet." "The Jews are publickly tolerated, and have their
Synagogue in *Amsterdam.* ... The *Catholicks* are the only [ones]
excluded from this liberty."[5]

Bishop Burnet recalled the acrimony of many of his countrymen in *History of His Own Time.* "Many mercenary Pens were
set on work to justify our Proceedings, and to defame our Allies,
more particularly the *Dutch;* this was done with much Art, but
with no regard to Truth, in a Pamphlet entitled the *Conduct of
the Allies* ... to which very full Answers were written, detecting
the Thread of Falshood [*sic*], that ran thro' that Work."[6]

These various British attitudes were not lost on the Dutch,
whose comments, although sometimes hostile, were, in general,
even-tempered. A sense of frustration over British intransigence
was clear in Willem Sewel's statement, "But I know that it is an
inborn characteristic of the English to be unwilling to learn from
foreigners; that's why they will not be grateful to me that I
venture to reprove them. ... " He was familiar with Dryden's
writings and said with some indignation that "... their famous
Dryden, ... was indeed a transcendent Wit, ... who was pleased
to call the Dutch heavy and gross-witted fellows. ..."[7]

A much more irate statement came in reaction to Swift's tract
The Conduct of the Allies. The Dutch commentator, in harmony
with Bishop Burnet's ideas, defended the need for a strong
alliance of England and Holland and belittled Swift's remarks.
He wrote, "Indien ik van die zelfden aard was als dien eerlyken
schryver, welke ik onlangs in handen Kreeg, mogt ik welde
gedaante van een overwinnaar aannemen ... dog wy zullen
niet meer door de lasteringen en valsheden van dien oneigenen
Schryver vervolgt worden."[8]

The mutual antipathy which had settled over both nations
might well have created irrevocable alienation, but unfortunate

and unwarranted expressions of division arising out of topical events were only superficial. Through long-established and profitable exchanges, these countries were irresistibly united by common interests in classical scholarship, in theology, in political theory, and in literature. Anglo-Dutch cultural relations remained relatively unimpaired as British and Dutch scholars, divines, writers, and politicians moved easily and confidently in each other's land, invigorating and fortifying the network of cultural ties.

I *Classical Scholarship*

The outstanding work of two generations of Dutch classical scholars was one of the greatest contributions to strengthening Anglo-Dutch cultural relations. In both countries, scholars working independently and often together, corresponding frequently and meeting occasionally, developed a strong communal interest in cutting away the underbrush of neglect which had stifled growth of humanity learning. In this field Dutch scholars led the way. The center of activity was Leyden, where Europe's most distinguished men found every encouragement. When Janus Dousa became curator of the newly founded university, one of his first acts was to persuade Justus Lipsius, the most famous scholar of his time, to settle in Leyden. The thrifty Dutch paid him well and asked of him little more than an occasional lecture. When he left in 1590, Dousa brought Julius Caesar Scaliger. Other distinguished classicists at Leyden were Claude Salmasius, Gerard John Vossius, Dominicus Baudius, Jan Meursius, and Hugo Grotius, whose works went far beyond Dutch boundaries.

On the other hand, in the same period British scholarship tended to be insular, with possible exceptions being the works of George Buchanan, John Seldon, and James Ussher, who were at the head of a limited roster of scholars whose writings enjoyed solid reputations abroad. More generally, the British concentrated heavily on historical scholarship and on the study of antiquity as these pertained to England. The second half of the seventeenth century witnessed a remarkable burgeoning of interest in Anglo-Saxon studies as well as in Anglo-Norman and English medieval history. While these subjects did not invite Continental interest on a wide scale, they were recognized on a local level.[9]

Before the Restoration the best scholarship was the product of such men as William Camden, Roger Dodsworth, William Dugdale, Sir Henry Spelman, and Francis Junius. Their efforts were well described by Sir Thomas Browne when he wrote in 1658, " 'Tis opportune to look back upon old Times, and contemplate our Forefathers.... The Supinity of elder days hath left so much in silence, or time hath so martyred the Records, that the most industrious Heads do finde no easie work to erect a new *Britannia*."[10] Yet, men of learning in both countries had much in common; their prodigious industry and intellectual stamina were equaled by their mastery of subjects. Dutch scholars were attracted to England and, as a result of visits, long stays and, in some cases, permanent settlement in London, greatly strengthened the bond between the two countries as the second generation of scholars prepared to continue the work of the first.

Seldom if ever has a scholarly and intellectual tradition been passed on to a new generation with so much assurance of its continuance. The great Dutch classical men of letters in the late seventeenth and early eighteenth centuries were in most cases sons, close relations, or prize pupils of the eminent leaders of the first generation. Isaac Vossius was the son of G. J. Vossius; Nicholas Heinsius continued the work of his illustrious father, Daniel; Ezechiel Spanheim's father had been a professor at Geneva and later at Leyden; Justus Scaliger was, of course, the son of Julius Caesar Scaliger; and, Jacob Gronovius inspired his son and namesake and Johann George Graevius. Jan van Broekhuyzen was always closely connected with Nicholas Heinsius and Pieter Burman encouraged his nephew, Pieter Burman, II. Like the first generation, the second found England an irresistible attraction and, consequently, many visited or lived in London. Isaac Vossius spent most of his life in England; Ezechiel Spanheim lived in London for many years.

On the other hand, the British could offer only Richard Bentley and, perhaps, William Wotton, Joshua Barnes, Joseph Wasse, John Davies, and Peter Needham. Of course, Bentley was the outstanding scholar and, no doubt, the most influential in Anglo-Dutch relations. From the British point of view, the second generation was the age of Bentley. His voluminous correspondence, collaborations, and academic quarrels were testimonials to cultural interchange between England and Holland.

During the seventeenth and the early eighteenth centuries,

Dutch scholarship was appreciated, used, but seldom praised in England. For example, when John Dryden and his colleagues translated Ovid's *Epistles* (1680), they used Borchard Cnipping's Dutch variorum, published in Amsterdam in 1670 which, in turn, had been based on Daniel Heinsius's earlier edition. Later, in 1693, Dryden remarked in *Examen Poeticum* that "not to follow the Dutch commentators always may be forgiven to a man who thinks them ... fit only to gloss on their own dull poets" and added, "But I leave a farther satire on their wit, till I have a better opportunity to shew how much I love and honour them."[11]

Like Dryden, Pope was content to rely on Dutch scholarship; he used Daniel Heinsius's edition of Horace, published at Leyden in 1629, as the basic text for the *Horatian Satires*. Yet he held Dutch scholars in general contempt. In *The Dunciad* he quoted from the "learned Scriblerus" on the matter of conjectural emendations. "Let it suffice, O Pallas! that every noble ancient, Greek or Roman, hath suffer'd the impertinent correction of every Dutch, German, and Switz Schoolmaster!" He added, "When these men have ceas'd to rail, let them not begin to do worse, to comment! Let them not conjecture into nonsense, correct out of all correctness, and restore into obscurity and confusion."[12]

Modern scholarship in both countries suffered at the hands of Swift and Pope. Not content with attacking the Dutch and other Continental scholars, Pope satirized Bentley's scholarship in the famous lines which still stand as an indictment of two generations of British and Dutch scholars.

> ... Since Man from beast by Words is known,
> Words are Man's province, Words we teach alone.
> When Reason doubtful, like the Samian letter,
> Points him two ways, the narrower is the better.
> Plac'd at the door of Learning, youth to guide,
> We never suffer it to stand too wide.
> To ask, to guess, to know, as they commence,
> As Fancy opens the quick springs of Sense,
> We ply the Memory, we load the brain,
> Bind rebel Wit, and double chain on chain,
> Confine the thought, to exercise the breath;
> And keep them in the pale of Words till death.[13]

In *The Battle of the Books* Swift attacked modern classical scholarship and claimed a quick victory, subjecting the vanquished to easy scorn and popular ridicule. His position is open to question and that of Pope is not completely true. The indisputable fact remains that Anglo-Dutch classical scholarship routed corrupt texts, solved many problems of allusion and explication, established more accurate chronology, and shared its learning with academic circles in British universities. Improved texts and necessary emendations benefited general readers, translators, paraphrasers, and adapters. For students, commentaries served as valuable guides through difficult passages; for translators, texts freed from corruption became essential tools. Despite the scorn of Swift and Pope, interest in the Classics was neither maimed nor destroyed; Dutch scholars had provided the vital force in the development and improvement of classical scholarship in the republic of letters.

II *Science and Theology*

In science, the British provided the thrust and the Dutch were the recipients. W. J. B. Pienaar pointed out that "Temperamentally the period was delivered over to politicians, intellectuals and virtuosi. There is no other time when English culture flowered into so much science and philosophy and so little *belles lettres.*"[14] The thoughts of Locke, Shaftesbury, Mandeville, Boyle, Newton, Wren, and of the Royal Society moved vigorously and quickly into Holland, where their fresh ideas formed the staple of the new philosophy, challenging and, subsequently, overthrowing the old. The movement was not completely one-sided; the Dutch contributed the work of Constantijn Huyghens, Boerhaave, Leuwenhoek, and a large roster of lesser known men who appear in the membership rolls of the Royal Society.[15] Mutual interests accelerated the burgeoning of the new science and this great fresh force of intellectual activity routed and finally destroyed old ideas and led to newer and more solid foundations for the advancement of scientific knowledge.

In theology the impetus was furnished by the Dutch. Although latitudinarian spirit and the dependence on reason grew equally well in both countries, the Dutch had been bolder and more forceful in their thinking and had been freer in publishing tracts which, in the opinion of conservative British clergymen, smacked of excessive license. Socinian works had been readily published in Holland under the direction of Etienne Courcelles,

professor in the Remonstrant college in Amsterdam, and were
becoming available in England. In *The Rehearsal Transpros'd*
(1672) Andrew Marvell considered such writings a threat. He
observed that "Socinian books are tolerated and well as openly
as the Bible." To orthodox British churchmen every Dutch
theologian seemed tainted with heresy and, at the least provocation, these clergymen exposed their fears. According to H. John
McLachlan, Holland had at that time become the main gate-
way through which Socinianism moved into England; the Dutch
were the "bridge situated between the rest of the Continent and
England, over which passed traffic of all kinds and, not least,
religious and cultural influences that had considerable repercussions and extensions on English soil."[16]

Orthodox British churchmen were more tolerant of latitudinarians and of Arminians than of Socinians. They saw a formidable
but not dangerous problem arising out of the close alliance of
sects stressing rational theology. Arminianism, Socinianism, and
rationalism of the Cambridge Platonists overlapped just enough
to form a fragile network, since all three emphasized reason over
inspiration or tradition. The close association of the Platonists
and the Arminians has now been recognized as an inevitability by
Aharon Lichtenstein, who has concluded that "the Platonists
and the Arminians had been moving along parallel paths, and
then, seeing that they were heading towards the same destination,
joined hands to make common cause."[17]

III   *Literature*

The general situation toward the end of the seventeenth century was not conducive to Anglo-Dutch interchanges in literature.
Earlier there had been strong links between writers in both
countries. Jacob Cats had visited England; Constantijn Huyghens
had translated some of Donne's poems into Dutch; and Vondel
had always shown great interest in British history. Conversely,
interest in the Dutch was evident in the writings of Evelyn, Pepys,
Temple, and Milton.

Literary estrangement at this time came as an outgrowth of
several factors: the unfortunate decline of Dutch literature after
Vondel; the growing aversion among the Dutch to read anything
in English except prose of a topical nature; the suspicion of
British poetical or fanciful writing; the unwillingness of the

British to learn Dutch; and the effective campaigns of the anti-Dutch pamphleteers. In reporting on this state of affairs in Holland, Willem Sewel wrote that there were "a number of English poets that do not interest Dutchmen, such as W. d'Avenant, J. Denham, J. Donne, B. Johnson [*sic*], J. Milton, J. Oldham, W. Shakespeare, Ph. Sidney, E. Spencer [*sic*], J. Suckling, E. Waller."[18] Theodor Weevers, in surveying the Dutch decline, noted that "the Dutch poets who wrote during the century after Vondel's death can no longer rank as poets of the Renaissance." Dutch poetry had lost its "freshness and flexibility" as the lesser poets of the new generation "were dazzled by the glamour of French classicism and regarded their Dutch predecessors, Vondel and Hooft included, as untutored talents who ... had not seen the light of taste and reason."[19]

In sharp contrast, during the same period British literature grew and, as a result, a strong literary current inevitably and eventually had to move from England to Holland. Thus, in the early eighteenth century the Dutch became increasingly aware of British literature and, by the third decade of the century, English literary figures were well known in Holland, as is evident through examination of Dutch *aucti-catalogi*.[20]

This very general overview of the more important strands of intellectual activity between the English and the Dutch indicates a community of interest more turbulent than harmonious. Differences of opinion could very easily have brought about total alienation, but essential general agreement among reasonable thinkers in both countries managed to maintain and even to strengthen their various bonds. Their points of agreement were: respect for the Classics; insistence on supremacy of Protestantism over Catholicism; belief in scientific progress; and resurgence of interest in literary matters. Disagreements arose mainly out of differences of national temperament. The English were conservative in approaching the Classics, sensitive to tampering with religious doctrinal interpretations, hesitant in disseminating learning and, in general, distrustful of too rapid cultural growth. The Dutch, on the other hand, were defiant in confronting the Classics, bold in theological argument, and zealous in popularizing knowledge of science and humanities. These differences were great but not irreconcilable; rather, they often acted as abrasives which polished and refined.

IV *The Dutch Republic of Letters*

But harmony as well as discord needs an intellectual market place. Fortunately for the history of Anglo-Dutch cultural relations, such a place was provided by the rapid and enduring growth of the periodical or journal, where all shades of controversy could be aired. These publications, dedicated to popularizing old and new books through reviews, abstracts and commentaries, were basically Dutch enterprises. As the seventeenth century moved into the eighteenth, the most influential of the journalists were Pierre Bayle, Basnage de Beauval, and Jean LeClerc, the great triumvirate of intermediaries. Their journals were destined to bring closer Anglo-Dutch relations and to give a pattern and a cogency to the multitude of variations in thought in both countries. Moreover, they were a convenient means for moving ideas far beyond the limits of cloisters, universities, and intellectual coteries; they became readily accessible in coffeeshops, in merchants' homes, and in bookstalls.

Bonds of common interest binding England and Holland might not have woven a strong fabric had it not been for the emergence of journalism, and journalism might not have won such quick and popular support had there not existed the encouraging atmosphere of the republic of letters. Here was an efficient and effective medium for intellectual exchange and for development of reciprocal support for new and often disturbing points of view. This remarkable milieu was the forum where British and Dutch theologians, philosophers, scientists, politicians, and scholars could exchange or introduce ideas. At its core was the firm commitment to increase knowledge, to eradicate superstition and to look for truth wherever it might exist. Acceptance of the need to search for truth whatever its source was a concept which automatically gave the republic of letters its cosmopolitan and international character. Too liberal for partisanship and too bold for orthodoxy, it found little favor among the conservatives but provided shelter for new ideas and a sympathetic audience for them.

Even the connotations behind the term, republic of letters, were those of opposition to the political status quo in the case of "republic" and of dissent against "literary" as distinct from "letters." Members of the republic of letters were in England, France, and Holland, but to account for its growth and longevity it seems essential to focus not on the French nor on the British but on the Dutch, whose important contributions have often been overlooked or ignored. Relative freedom from censorship, a general atmosphere of open inquiry, and the availability of many printers and booksellers in Holland combined to make that country the natural center of the republic. It is doubtful that London or Paris could have given it the physical and spiritual home necessary for survival.

The republic of letters was essentially without national identity but historians, writing from the point of view of a single country and limited by national pride, often failed to provide the impartiality which history demands. The republic of letters drew attention to the need for breaking down national barriers in order to permit a comprehensive, international view. It was the Dutch intellectuals who made great sacrifices to strengthen this movement; it was they who were willing to become denationalized for the sake of advancement of learning, as may be noted by the fact that they made special efforts to mask nationality by adopting Latin equivalents of their names. For example, Grotius is almost unrecognizable as De Groot; Vossius, as Vos; Dousa, as Van der Does; and, Perizonius as Voorbroek. Another important example in sacrifice of national identity was abandonment of their language and their yielding to Latin and to French. Dousa had questioned whether Dutch or Latin should be used for serious literary works and ultimately his question, apparently asked by others as well, led to Dutch becoming primarily a local medium of expression, fading into international obscurity as French and Latin (and to some extent English) replaced it. The Dutch language could well have maintained its place in the literary world as may be appreciated by the writings of Cats, Vondel, Hooft, and Revius, but unfortunately the Dutch chose to adopt a diffident attitude and to dub their language fit only for native use.

The international aspect inherent in a Dutch republic of letters raises the question of its true membership. Obviously, it is impossible to limit the constituency to native Dutch writers because thinkers and writers from other lands who spent their active lives in Holland were also involved. Notable examples are Pierre Bayle and Jean LeClerc. Bayle has always been identified as a Frenchman, living and writing in exile and yearning for a shift of affairs in France to permit his return there. Guy H. Dodge lists him among the Huguenots who remained loyal to Louis XIV, "from whose authority alone they expected their return to France. As a result they were hostile to William of Orange."[21] LeClerc, a Genevan by birth, always considered Amsterdam his home; the climate of intellectual Holland suited him perfectly. His praise of Amsterdam permeated much of his work. In *Bibliothèque Choisie* (Tome VI, Art. 5) he wrote, "It is an Honour to this Province, and to the Town of Amsterdam in particular, that it entertain'd and protected so illustrious a Refugee [as John Locke]. . . . May this Town ever remain a safe Sanctuary to the Innocent, and by its generous Carriage draw down upon itself the Praises and Blessings of all those who are Lovers of Virtue. . . . " And, of the republic of letters in Holland, he said that it was "a Country of Reason and Light, and not of Authority and implicit Faith, as it has been but too long."

Contemporary critics have discussed Holland's contribution. Pienaar wrote about the peril of denationalization and about the Dutch sacrifice in the cause of internationalism. But he also saw that these forfeitures amounted to "a virtue which had enabled them to absorb the finest qualities of the various types of foreign culture and enlightenment that lay beyond their borders."[22] In a forceful statement James W. Johnson bitterly assailed British xenophobia and lamented the deliberate ignoring of the Dutch. He concluded that "the extinction of the Dutch republic of letters, the real legacy and trust of Humanist learning, drew little interest and no laments in England, even among the later Neo-Classicists, whose ideals were derived from it and whose world-view was to perish with it."[23] J. A. Van der Welle saw British antipathy as mass envy and asked, "How must a nation of the power of Great Britain have felt, being surpassed in commerce and in other fields of activity by a country no bigger in all than a shire in England?"[24]

Despite sharp differences of national temperament, the Dutch spirit of cosmopolitanism prevailed and Anglo-Dutch cultural relations became the prime force in the republic of letters during the last decades of the seventeenth and the early decades of the eighteenth centuries. Removal of national barriers was in great measure due to the emergence of the journals in Holland. England contributed little but it was she who was the chief beneficiary; through the medium of these Dutch journals British thought was disseminated throughout Europe.

Pierre Bayle has been adequately considered within recent years; Basnage de Beauval still languishes in almost total obscurity; Jean LeClerc, the chief intermediary of this triumvirate, is vaguely remembered and only occasionally recognized. His journalistic output covered about fifty years; his work, independent of the journals, was widely read; his long and profitable association with the greatest British and Dutch thinkers of the period was unique and is well worth serious study.

V *Jean LeClerc's Identity*

Jean LeClerc, variously classified as a French exile, as a Huguenot, even as a Swiss theologian, still needs proper identification with the Dutch community in Amsterdam. Much of the confusion arises from his French name, from his association with French exiles in Holland, from his having gone from Geneva to Amsterdam during the mass movement of Huguenots from France and from his many works written in Latin and in French. Even in his own day he was well aware of his being improperly identified. Once he complained that some Englishmen confused him with the dissenter John Clark. English translators sometimes called him John LeClerc or John LeClerk.

In modern times the confusion persists and commentators do not wholly agree that he is Dutch. The problem is exemplified by the trio of French scholars who, in the 1930s, wrote on Anglo-Dutch and Anglo-French cultural matters during LeClerc's lifetime. Annie Barnes said that it was necessary to dissociate him from the French refugees and was on the verge of giving him outright Dutch nationality when she said, "Nul n'est prophète en son pays et LeClerc dut se consoler en se disant que la Hollande était devenue sa patrie."[25] Betty Morgan called him "un ... journaliste hollandais"[26] but also included Bayle in this category. Hilda Reesink simply placed LeClerc among the refugees.[27]

In England, Leslie Stephen referred to LeClerc and to Bayle as leaders of European criticism.[28] In France, Paul Hazard skirted the matter by merely calling LeClerc an "eminent critic ... whose *Gazette de Hollande* was a European organ of criticism...."[29] In the United States, Rosalie L. Colie first placed him among the French refugees but later implied that he really belonged in the Dutch community when she wrote of his role

as an intermediary in behalf of Ralph Cudworth and of his
close association with the Dutch theologian Philip van Limborch.[30] John J. Murray placed him well within the circle of
great Dutch intellectuals. "Amsterdam may not have contributed
as much to learning as some other cities, but it did provide an
intellectual climate for such men as Descartes, Locke, LeClerc
and Spinoza, to mention a few."[31]

Assignment of a writer to a particular country is not always
simple and clear-cut since neither place of birth nor of early
education can serve as arbitrary determinants for nationality
insofar as cultural history is concerned. The case in support of
LeClerc's being fixed solidly among the Dutch rests on many
facts. He spent all his productive years in Amsterdam, seldom
leaving that city; he never wished to return to his native Geneva.
Too, he maintained a life-long association with Dutch booksellers and kept steady contact with his Dutch friends, Wetstein,
Abraham van der Enden, Gisbert Cuper, and even with his
Dutch enemies, Pieter Burman and Joannes Vander Waeyen.
Most important of all, his close association with Philip van
Limborch placed the Dutch stamp upon his thinking.

More often than not, LeClerc extolled the virtues of the Dutch
and praised their ways of life. In a moment of despair, he once
wrote to Pierre Allix that "Les Hollandais n'ont que des défauts:
ils sont lents, froids et avares.... Ici l'avarice est considérée
comme une vertu."[32] But this sort of comment was the rare
exception. When he complained that the English language was
not well enough known in Holland, he said that such was the
case among "us"—meaning, of course, the Dutch.

He was Dutch because of his total integration into the mode of
thinking among the Dutch savants who insisted on use of reason,
on avoidance of obscurity, on systematic and even scientific
approach to exegesis, on general adherence to rules in critical
writing and on free and easy cultural exchanges. Jean LeClerc
was Dutch in everything but name and place of birth. It is
impossible to consider him stateless; it is inaccurate to deny him
his proper identity; it is unjust to diminish his stature in the
Dutch republic of letters.

CHAPTER 2

Biography

"He that would seriously set upon the search of truth ought in the first place to prepare his mind with a love of it. For he that loves it not will not take much pains to get it, nor be much concerned when he misses it."

I *The Earlier Years*

THE biography of Jean LeClerc as it relates to his accomplishments as scholar, critic, theologian, journalist, intermediary, and citizen in the Dutch republic of letters is essentially a recital of his writings and of his associations with the greatest minds in England and in Holland. His life was his work and his work, his life. Unlike Gerard Vossius, whose career has been described as "a quiet walk to the grave between two rows of ponderous folios,"[1] LeClerc's was a noisy battlefield on which he fought against the forces of ignorance, superstition, and prejudice. A bookish man in the best sense of the term, he was always in the vanguard of the endless battle for truth.

Born in Geneva on March 19, 1657, into a distinguished family, he early demonstrated his scholarly interests, recording that "He took so much Delight in Reading, that he was never Master of the Sports which Boys generally divert themselves with, and was likewise as unskilful in the Ludicrous Exercises of Youth."[2] He was aware of having a prodigious memory and a ready talent for turning out schoolboy verses. With faint irony, he wrote that he could have gained fame by courting the Muse, but preferred to concentrate on what he called "Things of a higher Concern" (p. 3).

In his father's excellent library he studied the Classics and when he was sixteen years of age undertook the study of philosophy with Robert Chouet, a "Gentleman of a singular way in Teaching" (p. 4), which signified that his mentor was

27

a follower of Descartes. A long and serious illness cut short his studies, but after recovery he began writing critical commentaries on the authors he was then reading. Two years of study in divinity and another in humanity learning prepared him for his career. From these early days until the end of his life he was "scarce ... without a Pen or a Book in his Hand for three Days"; scholarly work became "a second Nature" (p. 5).

His interest in divinity and his consequent awareness of religious intolerance even in Geneva made him eager to quit that city and in 1678, on the death of his father, he left for Grenoble to serve as tutor to the eldest son of the Counsellor N. Sarracen de la Pierre. His job demanded so little that he had ample time in which to continue his personal interests, but after a year he returned to Geneva, was admitted to Holy Orders and boasted that he "came off with extraordinary Applause in all his Examinations" (p. 7).

Although he had early developed an inclination to dissent from absolute authority in matters of religion, he did not subscribe to a definite creed until he read *Quaternio* by Stephen Curcellaeus, his paternal granduncle. This obscure work was his initial introduction to Arminianism and, once convinced of its basic tenets, he was determined to go to Holland where he hoped to pursue his new interests in a milieu more congenial to his independence of mind. However, before doing so, he spent a year in Saumur to improve his knowledge of French. In addition, he learned something far more important: In Saumur, such restrictions were placed on Arminianism that pastors were afraid to express their sentiments publicly. This state of affairs turned him irrevocably against the French. It was at this time that he began to correspond with Philip van Limborch, the foremost Arminian in Amsterdam, in order to clarify his own theological views.

Then he changed his plans again and went to London to learn English in order to understand some books written in that language and, as a guide, used Henry Hammond's *Practical Catechism* and his *Annotations on the New Testament*. LeClerc's facility in using the language progressed so rapidly that in a short time he could translate English into Latin. In addition, while there he preached in the French church and for six months was assistant to the Ministers in the Savoy. However, when he tried to become acquainted with British theologians, he was rebuffed. Such cold treatment probably arose from some of his sermons even though he insisted that he never preached anything that could be termed offensive, but there might have arisen some differences of opinion because "he generally argu'd from different Fundamentals than were us'd by others" (p. 11). He attributed the lack of warmth in the British to other reasons. "He paid . . . Visits to some Bishops and Doctors of the Church of *England*; but since he could not talk *English*, nor they *French*, except here and there one, and they were not willing to ingage in *Latin*, and besides [were] seldom so polite and courteous to Strangers as the *French*, he liv'd not long enough in *England*, to establish a Friendship with them" (p. 10). He added that he was leaving London because he was "offended with the Vapours, and Smoak of Sea-coal, which is the constant Firing us'd at *London*, so that he was in some fear least [sic] his Lungs were touch'd" (p. 11).

The defensive statement indicates that he had already become provocative and could not expect to find a moral and intellectual atmosphere in tune with his convictions in England any more than he had in France. As for the comment of the personal behavior of some British churchmen towards him, it is as unconvincing as is his remark on air pollution in London.

His London sojourn a fiasco, he left in company with Gregory Leti, who was moving to Holland after having been made unwelcome at the English Court.[3] LeClerc was determined to settle permanently in Holland, but before doing so he revisited Geneva. His mission was two-fold: to explain the reasons for his decision to his family and to try to persuade them to accompany him.

"I condemn not . . . those People who Dissent from my Opinion, and speak their Minds, tho' I disapprove [sic] their Sentiments; but it seems to me to be very unjust, to speak different from what one thinks. Nor is there scarce any thing more intolerable to a Lover of the *Truth*, or, what is all one, the Doctrine of that, which he takes for *Truth*, to hear it condemn'd and traduc'd in Pulpits, as a Thing of very dangerous Consequence; and the contrary Determinations strenuously asserted, while he has not so much as the Liberty of making a modest Reply. This is to betray and kick down the *Truth*, which would have been banish'd from the Earth, had they who first taught it been of such unaccountable Tempers. I will not attribute those

dangerous Consequences, which necessarily flow from some
Opinions, to those Men who would reject those Consequences,
tho' they admitted the Opinions from whence they arise: But
I think it in no wise the part of an Honest Man to be silent
of his Sentiments, the declaring of which seems to be the only
way of excluding those dangerous Consequences.

"My Case is different from theirs, who can speak what they
think, tho' they are in the wrong; and who live not as if they
would persuade the Consequences of their Doctrine, tho' they
should be admitted. For I am oblig'd to silence, tho' I hear all
manner of Contrarieties utter'd every where. Nay, I do not
esteem it safe to be silent, and dissemble my private Knowledge
of Things, because some fiery Bigots would pretend to find out
the Reason of my silence, and be ready to accuse me either
of Ignorance or Neglect, in not taking Notice of their Doctrine.
Wherefore, I take it to be much more advantageous for me,
without creating Trouble to my Friends and Relations, and
without injuring any one, to retire into *Holland* ... , where I
shall very willingly embrace any Opportunity of being instrumental to the Good of them, and Service of my Country"
(pp. 11-12).

LeClerc went to Amsterdam in 1683 where he began his
career by preaching a few sermons in the church of the
Arminians. The next year under the aegis of Van Limborch,
he started teaching "Philosophy, Humanity-Learning and the
Hebrew Tongue" (p. 12) at the college of the Arminians and,
for the next twenty-seven years, as professor of philosophy,
of humanity learning, and later of ecclesiastical history, he
devoted his time to his lectures and to the voluminous writings
which were to have a powerful influence on Anglo-Dutch
cultural relations. Ironically, he described all these years as
"that quiet State of Life, remote from all Ambition" (p. 12).

His career was studded with controversies with Dutch and
English disputants whose writings he believed were prejudiced,
excessively emotional, verbose, or obscure. Zest for battle appeared everywhere in his work overshadowing rare periods of
relative peace. He delighted in raillery but more often than not
it became only heavy-handed, vitriolic name-calling. "Slanderous
Scriblers," "ill-natured wits," "Renegados and Deserters from
the Holy Warfare" were typical epithets. He thought he was
a calm, reasonable, modest man who was sacrificing fame,

wealth, and leisure to work laboriously and without complaint because he took it "to be a Duty incumbent on every one, but especially those whom God [had] inabled [*sic*] to teach others; that they should leave no Stone unturn'd, to promote, as much as they can, Truth and Vertue" (p. 13). Such profession of humility holds more than a touch of irony. But even as he took pride in his work and expressed no strenuous regrets, he struck a note of disappointment when he confessed that he had "hop'd for greater Encouragement" (p. 12) to enjoy "the Ease and Pleasures of Life" (p. 13). He was disappointed never to have been "buoy'd up by the popular Breath" (p. 13) and with more than a trace of bitterness pointed out that he was "never assisted by the Smiles of Men in Power, nor advanc'd to any Offices in the Government" (p. 13).

When LeClerc was named professor at the university for the Remonstrants in 1684, he immediately began his work as an intermediary, editor, commentator, and critic. The first book was an edition of *Quaestiones Sacrae* (*Holy Questions*), written by an uncle, David LeClerc, a minister and erstwhile professor of Oriental languages in the University of Geneva. To it he added *Diatribae* (*Discourses*), written by another uncle, Stephen LeClerc, wrote a prefatory piece in which he "treated of the Lives of both" (p. 14) and included some annotations. In the same year he edited Charles le Ceno's *Theological Dialogues* and appended five dialogues.[4] Although these short pieces carried little importance, they show the direction which LeClerc's work was to take and reveal a vigorous and busy young man intent on making a quick and deep impression on the intellectual circles in Holland and in England.

At Saumur, he had read Father Simon's *Critical History of the Old Testament* and had seen that the author was "capable of being improv'd by some Additions" which might be of "Use and Satisfaction" (p. 16). After he had settled in Amsterdam, he saw a new edition of this work which gave him good reason to recall it and to further marshal his thoughts against it. Consequently, in 1685 he brought out *Sentimens de Quelques Théologiens de Hollande sur L'Histoire Critique du Vieux Testament*, a treatise of twenty letters in rebuttal of Father Simon's book. By use of the epistolary style, he was able to write with feigned indifference—as though he were simply the recorder of others' thoughts—but his handling of the *genre*

was faulty and its façade, easily pierced. LeClerc was readily
identified as the author; the attack was totally his. What he
had objected to mainly was Father Simon's reliance on conjectures rather than on facts and, therefore, he "used him
[Father Simon] with more than ordinary Freedom" (p. 17).

The book was destined to win a large measure of fame and
durability but its immediate effect was more profound than
LeClerc possibly could have anticipated. Its publication coincided with the early years of Locke's exile in Holland and when
Locke saw the book, he asked Philip van Limborch to introduce
him to the author. The meeting took place in 1685 and until
Locke's death in 1704, they enjoyed a vital and close relationship.

It is an easy and almost inevitable conjecture that their first
meeting led directly to *Bibliothèque Universelle et Historique,*
but there is no support for this assumption. Locke may have
agreed with LeClerc's suggestion for starting such a publication
but it is more likely that the young LeClerc had become increasingly impressed by the burgeoning journalistic writings and
saw opportunities for developing his career and for enhancing
his place in the Dutch republic of letters. To add to this was
the fact that Amsterdam booksellers, constantly on the lookout
for ways to increase sales, were favorably disposed to support
media already successful in reaching a new and growing reading public. Daniel de Sallo had brought out *Journal des Sçavans*
on January 5, 1665; The Royal Society had published the first
volume of *Philosophical Transactions* on March 6, 1665; *Acta
Eruditorum* had appeared in Leipzig in 1682; and Pierre Bayle
had started *Nouvelles de la République des Lettres* in March,
1684.

Now, Jean LeClerc joined the promising field by bringing
out the first issue of *Bibliothèque Universelle et Historique*
in January, 1686. His purpose was "faithfully to abridge some
Books which were every Day publish'd in *Latin, French, English,
Italian,* and *Dutch,*" and present abridgments "in such Words,
as may both want Obscurity, and ingage [sic] the Reader"
(pp. 18-19). From the very beginning he concentrated on books
by British writers and very soon had established himself as an
intermediary in the dissemination of British thought throughout
the Continent.

Although he wrote most of the journal, he still found time
to bring out several independent works which made him more

than simply a purveyor of the thoughts of others. After writing almost all of the first nineteen volumes and a good portion of those which appeared through 1691, he decided that the job of producing this periodical was too demanding. He disengaged himself from *Bibliothèque Universelle et Historique* and turned over his duties to Jacques Bernard, who was editor until 1693, when publication ceased upon the death of its bookseller and sponsor. At the time of his quitting, LeClerc had said that he needed time in which to write important and useful books and that he had experienced boredom and weariness from writing exclusively about modern writers.

Two events occurred, one in 1691 and the other in 1693, which may hold the real clue for his willingness to yield the editorship. On February 11, 1691, he married Mary Leti, daughter of the famous historian, and he may have wanted to lead a more leisurely life.[5] Two years later he ran into personal difficulty or disagreement with the Remonstrants in Amsterdam, who wanted to reduce his salary. As a matter of fact, the implications behind their action might well have been strong enough to convince him that he might be better off in England despite his earlier disappointment there.

The idea of a post among the British at this time was almost reasonable. After all, Pierre Allix had a good place at Salisbury; Pierre Du Moulin was fairly well situated at Canterbury; and Vossius and Casaubon had prospered in London. LeClerc's strongest hopes lay in his acquaintanceship with some of the more influential and powerful men. Burnet, Locke, Halifax, and even Addison were in favorable positions to help him secure a modest post and he actively solicited their advice and help. Yet with all these assets, LeClerc ran into obstacles from the very start and ultimately the entire project failed.

It is very possible that he had entertained the thought of making this move as far back as 1688. In that year he had seen Burnet appointed chaplain to Prince William; in February, 1689, Locke had returned home with the entourage of Queen Mary; and LeClerc was determined to maintain close contact with these two men he so highly admired. Possibly as a means for strengthening his ties with the British, in 1689 he brought out *Trois Sermons de Mr. Burnet* and in 1693 dedicated *Genesis* to Lord Pembroke, to whom Locke had already dedicated *An Essay Concerning Human Understanding*. Very likely Locke had suggested the potential worth of a dedication to Pembroke.

LeClerc had apparently disclosed to Burnet his wish to go to England and in a letter from Whitehall, dated January 29, 1696 (O.S.), Burnet tried to discourage him. "I never apprehended till of late that you did so much as desire to come to England. I thought the freedom in which you doe [sic] now live without being tied up by subscriptions and other practices might please your selfe tho with a narrow subsistance better then [sic] a larger provision that might oblige you to engagements and practices in which perhaps you would not be easy so you had no reason to blame me for not attempting that which I did not know you desired.... As for placing you in any of our Universities ... I dare not think you could live in them long with much quiet for the ... Calvinistical spirit begins to have a great operation among them and those who are known to have freer thoughts have little credit there and there is scarce any one thing that has brought me under more censure than that I have upon all occasions owned my friendship and esteem for you." Then, to conclude his discouraging letter and further dampen LeClerc's hopes, he wrote, "I will gladly contribute my endeavours to the procuring you a good settlement in England but I must tell you at the same time that it is not so easy a thing as you may perhaps imagine...."[6]

Locke was at the same time also involved in trying to do something for him. What may well have prompted Locke to move so insistently in LeClerc's behalf was a letter from Paul d'Aranda. In this letter, dated February 6, 1697, d'Aranda told of LeClerc's difficulties in Amsterdam and suggested that Locke participate in building a fund to help ease LeClerc's situation. Apparently Locke did not like the idea and initiated a more substantial plan by trying to get a permanent post for LeClerc either in England or in Ireland.[7]

Like Burnet, Locke was uneasy about LeClerc's controversial ways and the consequent unlikelihood of his finding a haven in England. But rather than drop the matter, he broached the subject to William Molyneux in Dublin. In a letter from Dublin on January 5, 1696/7, Molyneux wrote that he would like to know more about LeClerc, who had dedicated his *Ontology* to Locke and who had written *The Causes of Incredulity*. "To me he [LeClerc] seems an impartial and candid enquirer after truth, and [has] the true spirit of christianity in that his book.

The reason why I enquire after him, is, because I suppose him one of the refugees from *France,* and perhaps he may receive some encouragement to come into this Kingdom."[8]

On February 22, writing from Oates, Locke pursued Molyneux's suggestion regarding the possibility of LeClerc's moving to Ireland but hinted that there was still some hope of his settling in England and of this Locke wanted his Irish correspondent to say nothing. He thanked Molyneux for his concern for a "friend of mine in *Holland*" and vouched that LeClerc was "truly all that you think of him." Locke went on to say that a prebendary of about £200 per annum would be interesting to LeClerc because in Ireland he could have "a sure retreat to write in" and could be of "great use to the christian world."[9]

Molyneux replied on March 16 and indicated that while Locke knew of the hostility of the British clergy toward LeClerc and of his reputation as a powerful controversialist in church affairs, he had not perceived that the British attitudes had spread so swiftly to Ireland. He wrote that to find even a modest place for LeClerc was virtually an impossibility. "The clergy here have given that learned, pious, and candid man, a name that will frighten any bishop from serving him." Elaborating on the state of the clergy in Ireland, he continued, "I know but two or three that are in any post in the *church* capable to help him . . .; but, at the same time, I know them to be such cautious wary men, and so fearful of the censure of the rest of the tribe, that they would hardly be brought to it."[10] He reaffirmed his own high opinion of LeClerc and restated the fact that "an ecclesiastical preferment will be very difficult to be obtain'd for him."[11] He confessed that his original suggestion had been based on the belief that LeClerc was a single man, a refugee and "wholly unprovided for" and now regretted his ever having brought up the subject.

Notwithstanding, with good grace and determination, Molyneux persisted as far as he could on LeClerc's behalf. He introduced the subject to a clergyman identified only as "Dr. —— Dean of ——, a gentleman who is happy in your [Locke's] acquaintance." But this new intermediary "raised some farther scruples concerning Mr. *LeClerc's* ordination" and questioned "whether he would submit to those oaths, and subscription of assent and consent that are requisite thereto."[12] Molyneux re-

ported that the Dean would be in Holland in a few months
and would discuss the matter personally with LeClerc.

Then on July 20, 1697, Molyneux informed Locke that he
had broached the subject to still another clergyman, "the Bp.
of ——," who also raised the question of LeClerc's willingness
to take orders in the Church of Ireland and "to submit to the
oaths and injunctions thereof."[13] The letter concluded with a
request for Locke to try to learn how LeClerc felt about these
ecclesiastical formalities. Locke replied from London, September
11, 1697, that he had written to LeClerc but that he had not
yet heard from him.[14] By January, 1698, Locke still had had
no word and at this point the long correspondence ended. It
seems that Molyneux's interest faded as his health declined
and on his death in November, 1698, all possibility of LeClerc's
going to Ireland disappeared.

There does not seem to be anything which indicates that
had the Locke-Molyneux exchange been successful and had a
post been available for LeClerc in Ireland that he would have
taken it; there is no evidence that he had ever shown any
interest in going there. However, for a long time, even after
Locke's death, LeClerc persisted in enlisting the help of Englishmen; he was still determined to find a post in London.

Publication in 1708 of a volume of Molyneux-Locke correspondence made public the letters dealing with LeClerc. In
Bibliothèque Choisie, Tome 17, Article 6, 1709, LeClerc reviewed
this book and provided his own interpretation of the exchange—
one quite different from the facts. He made it appear that his
possible removal from Amsterdam had been Locke's idea but
that he had declined the invitation on the grounds that "l'état
tranquille, où je suis ici, n'est pas une choise, que l'on quitte si
facilement, pour ne pas parler d'autre raisons." But contrary
to what he had said in the review, he definitely had wanted
to go to England and had asked Joseph Addison to use his
influence with Lord Halifax. A letter from Addison to LeClerc
dated Whitehall, 23 May, 1707, reveals clearly the scope of
their correspondence on this subject.[15]

I am ashamed that I have not yet thank'd you for your kind
letter but I was unwilling to trouble you till I had seen my L.
Halifax who has bin [sic] so much taken up about the Scotch Union
and other publick Business that it has bin [sic] difficult to find an
opportunity of speaking with him. He call'd on me very lately and

told me that he had read over your letter and woud [*sic*] endeavour to manage that Affaire [*sic*] to your satisfaction. In the mean time he order'd me to present his Humble service to you and assure you that he will endeavour to serve you with all the secrecy that you desire. Perhaps It [*sic*] would not be amisse [*sic*] for you to write a letter of Acknowledgement to my L. Halifax and if you please to honour me with your Commands in relation to this or any other Business that you may have in England you shall always find me with great Zeal & Sincerity,

Your most Obedient and most Humble Servt.

J. Addison

Addison's extremely cautious, guarded, and discreet letter becomes clear in the light of what Joseph Wasse wrote to LeClerc in 1724. It seems that Lord Halifax with Addison as the intermediary had planned to install LeClerc as co-library keeper with Richard Bentley. Bentley, of course, considered this post his domain and would not tolerate any sort of partnership. Wasse intimated that Bentley thought LeClerc had initiated the idea and that Bentley's consequent harsh treatment of LeClerc arose from this incident. The upshot was, however, that Bentley was able to thwart even Lord Halifax because the plan never materialized. As Wasse put it, "The true reason [for Bentley's attack] was, that the Dr. receiv'd informations the then government intended to appoint you Co-librarykeeper with him, which he imagin'd was a thing of your seeking, and therefor coud [*sic*] not bear it; and that there was an intention of that sort, a Nobleman in the secret told me."[16]

This prolonged episode in LeClerc's life not only illuminates his steadfast admiration of the British but also throws a good deal of light on the strong conservative force which still dominated the Church of England. It further reveals surprising caution and even timidity on the part of Bishop Burnet and Joseph Addison to fight against innuendo, vague generalities, and sheer intellectual blindness rampant in conservative church circles. The efforts of Locke and Molyneux show them to have been more aggressive even though they were unable to overcome ingrained prejudice.

Insofar as LeClerc is concerned, it is perfectly clear that while feared by some as a dangerous man, he nevertheless was respected in high places and had become a powerful intermediary among the British. Over the years he had earned this reputation as a formidable controversialist through his books and journals which had flowed steadily from the Amsterdam booksellers. His writings had been translated quickly into English, had been published, and had been widely sold in London. The rapid success of *Bibliothèque Universelle et Historique* had brought his name to the attention of many important men in England.

LeClerc never turned his back on England; the disappointment had not diminished his admiration of the British as a nation of thinkers. Tangible evidence is seen in his dedications to Pembroke, Shaftesbury, Sunderland, Sharp, Tennison, Wake, and Burnet.

II *His Works*

By its sheer bulk, Jean LeClerc's work is overwhelming. He had once bragged—and with good reason—that he had written more books than some would-be scholars had read. His writings for the most part dealt with treatment and exposure of what was going on in England—matters of lively interest among contemporary readers concerned with the increasing flow of new ideas. His books were a well-equipped repository of the exciting intellectual times and became part of the massive web of thought binding England and Holland. This was a period when the trimmer was held in contempt and when men took sides with a passion belying the strong vogue for reason and good humor. In such an atmosphere LeClerc felt at home and occupied an important place in the international and cosmopolitan Dutch republic of letters. A summary of his more valuable works should illustrate his force, his range and his impact on the thinking of his day as well as the importance of his role as an intermediary.

In 1688 and in 1689 he translated into French three sermons by Bishop Burnet which had been written on the occasion of William and Mary's accession to the throne. At about the same time LeClerc joined forces with Burnet against Varillas, whose *History of the Changes of Religion* "feign'd many Things relating to the Reformation in *England*."[17] He translated Burnet's *Confutation and Defence against the Ninth Book of Varillas's History* and to support Burnet, wrote a strong preface against Varillas's reliance on conjecture and on his use of unauthenticated history.

In 1690 he revised and corrected Louis Moreri's popular *Dictionnaire Historique* in an effort to rid it of many faults. Although he complained of the lack of time to write a complete revision and of paucity of sufficient reference books for the task, he amended "some thousand of Errors, which were obvious to him in his cursory Reading" (p. 25). LeClerc reported that his revised dictionary was so popular in Holland that in twenty years almost 10,000 copies of it had been sold there. Part of his interest in this work had grown out of his wish to rival, if not to eclipse, Bayle's tremendously influential dictionary, about which LeClerc said in justification of his revision, "For why should not a Dictionary, which has those things in view, [truth, religion and virtue] do as much good as BAYLE's did harm...?" (p. 26).

Busy as he was with the periodical, the translations of Burnet, and the revision of Moreri's dictionary, he faithfully attended to his professorial duties. When he found no suitable texts for students, he wrote his own. Accordingly, he brought out *Logic, Ontology,* and *Pneumatology* "that he might have a Treatise of his own, by which to explain his Mind to his Scholars" (p. 21). Published at Amsterdam in 1692, *Logic* was dedicated to Robert Boyle and the other two to John Locke. The dedication to Boyle is noteworthy since LeClerc, representing contemporary opinion, praised Boyle less as a scientist and more as a philosopher. Boyle died before he had received a copy and in 1697 LeClerc dedicated the second editions of all three to Locke.

Logic emphasized LeClerc's adherence to the use of right reason everywhere. He pointed out that "It is a grievous Injury to the Christian Religion,... when they [the poorly instructed] deny, that we ought to give any heed to Reason in Matters which concern Religion.... For, while in every Thing else they allow themselves the use of Reason,... yet, when we come to talk of Religion,... they continually suspect some Fallacy" (pp. 21-22). The text, essentially dealing with theology, argued in favor of the use of logic to disclose and to rout sophistry in religious writings. *Ontology* was designed to help his students understand "the way of speaking which those Divines made use of, and also by Degrees learn how to use the Axioms, which were eternally true, to Purposes of a higher Importance" (p. 22). *Pneumatology* was essentially a clarification of his own limited dependence upon Cartesianism. He pointed out as often as possible where he ran counter to Descartes's ideas, especially in his arguments on "God's Power to change the Essences of Things" and on his commentary dealing with "the Possible and Impossible . . . [to depend] on the mere Divine Will" (p. 23).

Between 1693 and 1695 LeClerc concentrated on biblical studies which resulted in commentaries on *Genesis, Exodus, Leviticus, Numbers,* and *Deuteronomy.* These lengthy studies, written in Latin, were followed by *Paraphrases and Notes on the Beginning of St. John's Gospel* which was eventually printed as part of *Pentateuch.* This work is of special interest because in it LeClerc, apparently in self-defense, emphasized that his paraphrase "utterly overthrows the Doctrine of the UNITARIANS" (p. 26). He had been forced into this position because he was disturbed by the increasing frequency in which his work was "blasted with the odious Name of SOCINIANISM" (p. 27).

Following these biblical studies, he returned to writing for the benefit of his students. In 1695 there appeared *Physica* and in 1696, *Ars Critica.* The first was a hodge-podge of modern and outdated notions of which his critics rightly complained. Lynn Thorndike has described *Physica* as "an odd jumble of authorities, citing Newton as to comets and tides . . . yet still quoting Pliny . . . as to gold, silver and salts." Yet he is sympathetic in his conclusion that "on the whole, although LeClerc may have failed to sketch a complete and consistent system or to discover fundamental principles of physical science, he does provide a not unfair reflection and retrospect of the ups and downs, the change and confusion, the back currents and the stream of progress, in the scientific thought of the seventeenth century."[18]

The first part of *Ars Critica* was meant to prepare young scholars to undertake classical studies after mastery of ancient languages. The second section considered chiefly the problem of "distinguishing the spurious Places and Writings from the genuine" and the making of "a Judgment of the Style and Character of an Author" (p. 28).

Ars Critica and *Physica* became established texts in Holland, more especially in England and, surprisingly, in America. At Cambridge University *Physica* was among the texts used by generations of students and at Harvard College *Ars Critica* was long used. Their remarkable longevity illustrates LeClerc's influence on academic thinking not only in his own day but for at least two hundred years longer. In his bibliographical study, *The Cambridge University Press 1696-1712,* D. F. Mc-Kenzie has recorded that the University Press printed a fifth edition of *Physica* in 1700, a sixth in 1704, and a seventh in 1708. The fifth and sixth had consisted of 750 copies each and the seventh, of 1,000 copies. He noted further that the 1704 edition of the trilogy, *Logic, Ontology,* and *Pneumatology,* had been printed for the use of students of moral philosophy and metaphysics.[19]

When the Harvard Divinity School was established in 1816, *Ars Critica* was used as a standard text.[20] Charles Andrew Farley translated parts of it in the 1830s and the University Press at Harvard printed only the section of Part II which dealt with "Signification of Words and Phrases" and with "General Principles of Interpretation."[21]

LeClerc's academic texts have been overshadowed by his more comprehensive works which were of interest to a wider reading public. During the first fifteen years of his career he dealt with disputatious, argumentative material and thereby earned the warranted reputation of a stubborn commentator, an impatient critic, and a willing disputant.

The success of *Bibliothèque Universelle et Historique* and his growing reputation after quitting the journal convinced Henri Schelte, the Amsterdam bookseller, that another journal by LeClerc could prosper. Accordingly, in 1703 LeClerc began publication of *Bibliothèque Choisie.* In a prefatory note he said that here he would write not only about modern books but also about "ancient books, as they come into my hands without order or the time in which they appeared. I will make exact resumés and I will speak what I think of them." He had become aware of the existence of a growing class of readers who were anxious to know more about the activities of the republic of letters and his goal was to reach this audience heretofore apparently ignored or overlooked. "This work," he announced, "is not for the ignorant nor for the 'savants.' It is for those who don't have time to read everything they'd like to. It is also for young people just getting a taste for study." In a few years the same idea would lead to the journalistic efforts of Addison and Steele, but LeClerc was among the first to recognize the need for pleasing as well as instructing this general readership.

By thus widening his scope, LeClerc was free to roam everywhere in the world of books. *Bibliothèque Choisie* was studded with reviews, resumés, and commentaries on such important writers as Nehemiah Grew, Ralph Cudworth, Thomas Rymer, Joseph Addison, the third Earl of Shaftesbury, Richard Bentley, and John Tillotson, to name only the more well known. In balancing measure, he dealt with such eminent Dutchmen as Anthony van Dale, Pieter Burman, David Hoogstraat, Frederic Gronovius, Janus Rutgers, Jan Broekhuyzen, Burcher de Volder, Tiberius Hemsterhuis (father of the Dutch philosopher, Franciscus Hemsterhuis), and others. French writers were deliberately ignored because, he said, "tout le monde peut les lire, aussi bien que moi, et s'en former une juste idée."[22]

Bibliothèque Choisie continued without interruption through twenty-seven tomes, ending in 1713 with the death of the bookseller. According to LeClerc, another reason for its cessation was his need for more time to work on commentaries on the Old Testament and on ecclesiastical history as it pertained to the first six centuries of Christianity. But again he did not have time for these projects because, in 1714 David Mortier, another enterprising Amsterdam bookseller, persuaded him to undertake a continuation of *Bibliothèque Choisie* under the title *Bibliothèque Ancienne et Moderne*. This third journal had a life of thirteen years during which period LeClerc continued publicizing British writers, notably Isaac Newton, Addison and Steele, and such lesser ones as Thomas Cockman, Zacharias Pearce, John Davies, Joseph Wasse, and Joshua Barnes. In this journal Dutch writers were deliberately ignored but in this case LeClerc never gave a reason. He often mentioned new works by his countrymen but refrained from giving them the copious treatment he accorded those of the British.

Bibliothèque Ancienne et Moderne ran its course and, finally, LeClerc returned to his unfinished work. He said, "I have often thought for several years to quit the job of the Bibliothèque in order to finish my commentary on the Old Testament which I started as long ago as 1693." Now he kept to his word and, rid of journalism, finished this project in about two years.

The two *Bibliothèques* which had spanned the years between 1703 and 1727 had not taken all his time and energy; it seems that they had served essentially as background for other writings.

For example, he wrote the text on natural philosophy to complete the third and fourth volumes of *Philosophical Works*. Further revisions were needed on Moreri's *Dictionnaire Historique* and he had labored over them "even to the Ninth Edition, which came out in 1702" (p. 25).

In 1696 there appeared the treatise *Of the Benefit and Blank Tickets,* dealing with lotteries which were then beginning to be established in Holland. He argued against the use of such "senseless Terms" as *Benefit* and *Blank* and observed that "the Divine Providence is not preternaturally consider'd in the common Lots" (p. 29). Of a second work during this year, *The Causes of Incredulity,* it was reported that he had told friends that "if he had any Parts, Wit or Judgment, however small it was [*sic*], he had laid it all out in Writing that little Treatise" (p. 30).

With the amazing industry which characterized his whole career, LeClerc continued substantial publication. In 1697 there were *Compendium of History,* a chronology for student use; in 1698, the well-known *Annotations on the New Testament* by Henry Hammond, a work destined to provoke hostility among Dutch and English critics; in 1699, *Parrhasiana,* a series of informal essays in which he expressed his ideas on various and general topics—poetry, true and false eloquence, historiography, the differences between ancient and modern historians, and the decay of contemporary learning. He included a long, exhaustive defense of his own works. *Parrhasiana,* as will be seen, became one of his most popular works; it was the main gate through which the reader could penetrate into some of LeClerc's basic ideas. Of no less value it serves to show his power and influence as an Anglo-Dutch intermediary. The popularity of this miscellany was so great that he was prompted to write a sequel but it did not attain the success of the original. Somehow, the zest, the liveliness, and the force of the first were never duplicated in the second even though he dealt with important topics such as how to make a republic happy, how to differentiate between true and false zeal, and how to consider friendship.

LeClerc now turned his attention to classical scholarship and within a few years brought out new editions of Petavius, Hesiod's *Theogonia,* Albinovanus, and Servius. For each he supplied a preface and notes and, since he had leaned heavily on earlier

Dutch scholars in an effort to equal or even to surpass their excellent work, he put himself in the mainstream of Dutch classical scholarship. His chief purpose had been to produce editions which removed obscurities, explicated difficult passages, or refined texts, but he had also managed to place his individual stamp on each of these works.

The edition of Petavius, written under the pseudonym "Theophilus Alethin, S.J.A.E.," was noteworthy for its preface, a digressive essay in which he found fault with John Martinaeus's interpretation of St. Jerome. LeClerc resolved his differences with this Benedictine monk by writing *Quaestiones Hieronymianae*.

His involvement in the new edition of Hesiod's *Theogonia* was a curious collaboration with Graevius and illustrates the bickering which pestered Dutch classical scholarship. At the request of the bookseller, LeClerc had combined in a single edition his own notes with those of Graevius. Both men had long been friends, had corresponded frequently, and had even exchanged books. They had discussed this edition and had agreed that Graevius's notes would be placed at the beginning of the last volume and LeClerc's at the beginning of the first. Evidently LeClerc was the more active participant, because when he had read Graevius's notes, he found them filled with "many *Arcana* of Fabulous History" (p. 38) and, tactlessly, tampered with them. At about the same time Graevius had written a friendly letter to LeClerc, but at the close had expressed displeasure with some passages in *Parrhasiana*. "I wish some things had not been said in your *Parrhasiana*, not for the sake of others, but yourself, whom I have in the greatest Esteem."[23]

Graevius was nettled by LeClerc's handling of his notes and LeClerc was annoyed by Graevius's disapproval of passages in *Parrhasiana* and these slight differences led to a cooling of their friendship. LeClerc found a good opportunity to belittle Graevius when he wrote a prefatory essay on etymology for Matthias Martinius's glossary of Isidorus, which had been embellished with notes by Graevius. The bookseller had asked LeClerc to write a preface in the hope of revitalizing a work which had not sold well. Recalling this edition, LeClerc said that "the Book went off much easier afterward, which otherwise had been condemn'd to Oblivion" (p. 39). Then, with malice or irony, he added, "There was some Merit in the Work it self;

and, being beautified by GRAEVIUS's Addition, was well worth the buying" (p. 39). He took full credit for reviving the work by emphasizing that his essay was absolutely essential for "many, who knew not the Use of Etymologies, [and] might be set to rights by the Preface" (p. 39). Such displays of vanity and quibbling undermined the foundations of classical studies and hindered progress. LeClerc saw clearly that these exchanges were a contributing factor to the decay of humanity learning but, like many of his Dutch colleagues, he was blind to his own faults and was, himself, instrumental in hastening the decay he deplored.

The editions of Albinovanus and of Servius, brought out for his students and for the learned community, appeared under the pseudonym "Theodore Gorallus." This name is a playful disguise when it is recalled that *Goral* derives from the Hebrew word for "minister." Both editions may well be passed over except for their prefaces, in which he scolded some scholars whose editions of classical works contained only "Emendations from Books of meer Conjectures" (p. 40) and who deliberately ignored difficult passages which needed explication. He charged that their silence did not so much betray their poor learning as it hid their ignorance. Here again is an example of a blunt attack on irresponsible scholarship. As good editors he offered Scaliger, Lipsius, and Isaac Casaubon.

Following this excursion into the classical world, LeClerc returned to biblical writing and to a new edition of the works of Erasmus. In 1703 his French translation, with notes, of the New Testament came out and was vigorously attacked both at home and in England. He had invited controversy by disclosing that his translation had brought into the open the obscurantism of some clergymen who, in reply, could only accuse him of being a Socinian. A long admirer of Erasmus, he had seen the need for a new edition of his countryman's work and, early in the same year, he brought out the first volume and over a period of three years, others, so that by 1706, this monumental edition had been completed. It was, admitted LeClerc, really his tribute to the memory of Erasmus for whom he "had always an Affection," calling him "this Second Eye of *Holland*" (p. 50). For him, as ever, Hugo Grotius always remained the "First Eye." In the account of his own life, LeClerc digressed to comment fully on Erasmus and on this edition.

After praising him as a scholar and as a theologian, he added a spirited defense of Erasmus's actions in attacking his critics and those "who were addicted to the *See* of *Rome*" (p. 54). LeClerc believed that his greatest service was to put the various parts in proper chronology. Heretofore, because there were no dates or only erroneous ones, Erasmus's thoughts had been imperfectly understood.

The heavy accumulation of writings, overwhelming in volume and in range, had made LeClerc the most popular and most widely read Dutch writer. His work was acclaimed, attacked, discussed, vilified, but never ignored. Whatever he wrote either in his *Bibliothèques* or in his independent writings created excitement.

III *The Gabillon Imposture*

A singular event which began in 1707 and continued through most of 1708 provides an accurate measure of LeClerc's fame, importance, and popularity in England. Rumors had spread that he had been visiting in England, but when it had been established that he had never left Amsterdam, an investigation revealed that one Auguste de Gabillon, posing as LeClerc, had successfully duped several English churchmen and others. He was exposed by Jacques Bernard's notice in *Nouvelles de la République des Lettres* (Article VI, November, 1707). Bernard's British correspondent (probably Pierre Desmaiseaux) had written a general account of Gabillon's cheating a bookseller who had extended credit to him believing him to be LeClerc.

When LeClerc heard of the imposture, he wrote to John Chamberlayne, Justice of the Peace for the City and Liberties of Westminister, on November 10, 1707, asking for more news. On November 25, Chamberlayne replied with a long, detailed account of Gabillon's activities.[24] He told how Gabillon had attended a Sunday service in Essex and had so impressed the parson that he had been invited to dinner. During the visit, Gabillon asked his host if he knew Jean LeClerc. When the parson said that he had never met him but that he had heard a great deal about him and had read some of his works, Gabillon announced that he was LeClerc and that he was in England to persuade churchmen that "there was nothing in his writings dissonant from the doctrine of their Church." Having satisfied the parson of his credentials, Gabillon told of his influence with the Duke of Ormond and said that in appreciation for all the hospitality he had received, he would see the Duke in order to get a better benefice for him. The parson was so dazzled by the prospect of advancement, he gave Gabillon a substantial amount of money, ". . . but being soon after undeceived," wrote Chamberlayne, "[he] too late repented his fond Credulity."

Encouraged with the success of this prank, Gabillon "rambled from one Minister's house to another and received abundance of . . . good entertainment from them all." Then, to show his appreciation, he invited his genial hosts to a "splendid Dinner" at a tavern in Rumford. According to Chamberlayne's report, after "having entertained them with plenty of Wine and good Victuals and Night coming on he privately slipt away, and left them all in pawn for the reckoning."

In the same letter to LeClerc, Chamberlayne told of Gabillon's swindling a minister named Cigala out of eight or ten pounds by promising to persuade the Archbishop of London to give the impoverished minister a good post. Without going into detail, Chamberlayne added more about Gabillon's actions by mentioning "how he cheated a Bookseller of a large Sum of money; how he behaved himself at Baron Schuss [*sic*] house the Hannover Envoys, and many others of his pranks."

By April 30, 1708, Chamberlayne had issued a formal complaint vouching for the truth of the information he had given "some time ago to the Reverend Mr. LeClerc Minister at Amsterdam in one or more Letters touching the Rogueries & Imposture of one Gabillon, formerly a monk of the Theatin Order at Paris, now a Pretended Proselyte in Holland." To add support to his charges, he obtained a certificate from the Archbishop of London.[25] In his certificate, the Archbishop told an amazing tale of Gabillon's temerity in attempting to extract money from the Queen to support his work in connection with a report on the present state of England—a report which the Dutch government had requested. Doubtful of Gabillon's credentials, the Queen had delayed making her decision and, during the waiting period, news had reached the Court of his misconduct in Holland, his trouble with creditors and his "feigned Storyes & pretences." When Gabillon realized that his scheme was doomed, he hurriedly quit London intending to take the boat at Harwich for Holland and en route engaged in the

escapades and in the mischief which Chamberlayne had related
to LeClerc. The Archbishop's certificate noting that Gabillon
had "cheated several people by the Way, & pretended to some
of the Clergy, that he was Monsieur LeClerc" seems to be a
general statement confirming Chamberlayne's detailed account.

In the April, 1708, issue of his journal, Bernard continued
his exposure of Gabillon by summarizing a pamphlet entitled
*Lettre à Mr. Bernard &c, sur l'Apologie de Frédéric Auguste
Gabillon, Moine défroqué*, printed in Amsterdam for Henri
Schelte (1708). The anonymous pamphleteer had supported
Bernard's earlier article by citing the account of the imposture
which had been printed in Boyer's *Post-Boy* and by recalling
the testimony of one Mr. Whitaker, identified and described
as "Sergent aux Loix très-habile Jurisconsulte et d'une probité
connue."

The most vivid account of Gabillon's imposture is in a letter
dated May 3, 1708, from d'Origny de la Loge, a member of
the staff of the Duke of Essex at Woodford, to Pierre Desmaiseaux.[26] D'Origny recounted that as he was strolling near
his house, he was approached by a handsome man wearing a
blond wig, a black coat over a damask vest, and a hat with a
rose attached. The stranger asked if this was the estate of the
Duke of Essex and inquired if it was possible to meet him.
When told that the Duke was not at home, Gabillon began his
imposture by asking d'Origny if he knew him and when d'Origny
said that he had never seen him before, Gabillon announced
that he was LeClerc.

"Je lui répondit que je connoissoit son nom fameuse par ses
ouvrages estimois et honoroit...," said d'Origny. Gabillon accepted the high praise of LeClerc's work and then confided that
he was traveling incognito to Cambridge, where he was to
become professor of oriental languages and asked that the
matter be kept secret.

D'Origny invited him to breakfast but the visit lasted all day.
During the prolonged conversation, Gabillon asked if he had
any manuscript worthy of publication and d'Origny produced
a work which he described as "un petit ouvrage... melé de
vers et de prose françoise de ma façon sous le titre de lettre
écrite Des champs Elisez par l'ombre de M. Le Marquis...
de Corbinelli." Gabillon liked it and d'Origny produced another,
a new critique of Telemachus, which also was highly praised.

Gabillon insisted on taking them so that he could print them in *Bibliothèque Choisie* and promised to return the manuscripts on his way back from Cambridge. Later, during a visit to London, d'Origny heard about the imposter and in his letter to Desmaiseaux asserted that he was sure that he also was one of Gabillon's victims.

Chamberlayne's charges had been circulated and Gabillon demanded an apology and a retraction.[27] On June 5, 1708, he wrote of his astonishment at the charges brought against him in view of the fact that Chamberlayne had been most cordial to him during his London sojourn, but his letter did not enumerate specific charges which he believed untrue or damaging. Chamberlayne's reply mentioned that he had a packet from LeClerc containing "a Latin Paper supposed to be writ" by Gabillon, entitled *Apology,* and he now asked Gabillon to be specific about the charges to which he objected.[28] When he received them, there would be forthcoming "a very full answer by the next post."

". . . if it shall appear that I have wrong'd you in any thing that I have writ to Mr. leClerc about you, for I have writ to him several times upon the Topic of your personating him here in England . . . I will go a thousand Miles most willingly to doe you right since I wish nothing more than that you should make appear your Innocence as Great as you pretend it, . . .," wrote Chamberlayne.

Again, on June 25, 1708, he wrote to Gabillon, challenging him to vindicate himself in view of the damaging evidence presented by the Archbishop of London, by Mr. Whitaker, and by d'Origny de la Loge.[29] From this letter, it seems that Gabillon had previously written in self-defense that LeClerc had altered Chamberlayne's certificate. Chamberlayne protested. "I shall most firmly abide by any Certificate of mine that the Reverent [*sic*] M^r LeClerc has thought fit to publish, even without collating it with the Original, . . . if he were capable of altering anything in my aforemention'd Certificate, of which business I will never suspect him guilty."

Gabillon never returned to England to defend himself and the whole matter seems to have been dropped. However, there were minor repercussions which pleased LeClerc. The unmasking of Gabillon served to destroy the latter's credibility and, at the same time, to utterly devalue his attack on LeClerc's commentaries on the *New Testament*. In 1707 there was printed a treatise entitled *La Defense de La Divinité de Jesus-Christ et De la Grace intérieure, par L'Ecriture Sainte contre Les Paradoxes Impies et extravagans de M. Le Clerc. Et de ses adherens, avec La Refutation De ses Notes sur le Nouveau Testament.* This work, according to the title page, was printed in The Hague at the expense of its author. In the preface, Gabillon recalled a chance meeting with LeClerc at a bookseller's in Amsterdam and remembered that LeClerc had told him that he cared neither for his method of discussion because he was too filled with sophisms and classroom subtleties nor for his overheated manner of debate. Gabillon countered that his warmth and his enthusiasm came from his zeal to defend his religion. Since Gabillon was no match for LeClerc, the best he could do by way of refutation was to inform his readers that LeClerc was "un socinien outré" and a "Ministre Arminien."

LeClerc commented ironically and with evident pleasure that the imposture had been "a great Grief to him, that some of the most ingenious Men were deluded by an Imposter, which he was no wise concern'd in; but yet it was a means to him to return Thanks to those Learned and Good Men, who were deluded by such a Report, because he perceiv'd that they paid a Compliment even to a Cheat, who disguis'd himself under his Name."[30]

IV *The Later Years*

On April 30, 1712, Philip van Limborch died. He had been LeClerc's mentor and guide since 1683, had been chiefly responsible for his career among the Remonstrants in Amsterdam, and had been the link between him and Locke. The funeral oration which LeClerc delivered on May 6 was printed in *Bibliothèque Choisie* (Tome XXIV, Part 2) and, early in 1713, was translated and published in England.[31] The eulogy was distinguished for its emphasis on Van Limborch's relationship with Locke. LeClerc lauded Van Limborch's advocacy of the use of reason and moderation in serious discussion and on his insistence that zealots "are to be oppos'd with Gentleness and Arguments, and not with ill Language and Rage" (p. 26).

In 1712 LeClerc was named professor of ecclesiastical history, and on September 6, he delivered the traditional oration which,

like so many of his other writings, was quickly translated into
English. In it he had pointed out that history serves a moral
purpose by promoting peace but that ecclesiastical history
has a special problem because "no Christian Society ... agrees
in all things with the Fathers, either separately or united in
Council."[32] At the same time he engaged in academic wrangling
with Richard Bentley and Pieter Burman. What they fought
over is now of little interest but casts strong light on the fervor
and energy expended on acrimony in the early decades of the
eighteenth century.

The dispute with Bentley started in 1709 when LeClerc found
fault with his critical notes in John Davies's edition of Cicero's
Tusculan Disputations.[33] Then, after Bentley had read LeClerc's
edition of Menander and Philemon, their quarrel became heated.
Taking full advantage of his powerful and remarkable scholarship, Bentley tore LeClerc's work to pieces. According to R. C.
Jebb, "Bentley wrote his own emendations on 323 of the
fragments. He restored them metrically, showing that LeClerc
had mixed them with words from the prose texts in which
they occur, and had then cut the compound into lengths of
twelve syllables, regardless of scansion."[34] To give his criticism
added sting, Bentley persuaded Pieter Burman of Utrecht to
publish the emendations under the pseudonym Lipsensi Phila-
leutherus. Burman, at this time already engaged in a bitter
quarrel with LeClerc, welcomed the opportunity to further
humiliate him.

A belated review of an edition of Horace brought out in 1696
by "Les Directeurs de l'Académie de Cambridge" in *Bibliothèque
Choisie* (Tome III, Article 4), praised Bentley's emendation of
male Tornatos to *male Ter Natos* (verse 441 in *Ars Poetica*)
and added the hopeful note that another edition of Horace
would be valuable "avec des notes de cet habile homme, où
il y aura sans doute bien d'autres passages corrigez et éclaircis
d'une manière nouvelle." Very soon after this review, Bentley
brought out an edition of Horace, and immediately after its
publication in Cambridge and in Amsterdam, LeClerc wrote
a long commentary in which he indicted Bentley for straying
from reason and for resorting to "a happy Sagacity in *Divination*
and Conjecture" in his attempt to remove textual corruptions.[35]
He reminded Bentley that intermingling of conjecture and evidence was "Prejudicial to the Art of Reasoning justly and exactly."

With good grace he admitted to his own misuse of conjecture in
the edition of fragments from Menander and Philemon and put
himself on the same level as Bentley by calling their mutual
defect the "Weakness and Imperfections of a Humane Mind."[36]
But LeClerc recognized Bentley's superiority as a scholar and
closed the matter by announcing that he had always admitted
when he was wrong.

The effects of the Bentley-LeClerc controversy spilled over
into the much more vitriolic one between Burman and LeClerc.
Bentley's use of Burman had intensified a dispute which should
never have occurred. What had enraged LeClerc was that Burman, in the preface to his edition of Petronius Arbiter, had
attacked him for denigrating Graevius. Burman had satirized
LeClerc as far back as 1703 in *Dialogue de Spudaeus et de
Gorallus* for what he believed to be shabby treatment of
Graevius's editorial work and had been angered by LeClerc's
statement that Graevius was neither so erudite as Scaliger nor
so painstaking as Gruter. Among other things, Burman had
called LeClerc a mercenary of the booksellers. LeClerc had
replied that what a man of letters can earn from a Dutch
bookseller is so small that it is not worth talking about. Then
Burman had called. him a foreigner among the Dutch and
LeClerc had reminded the Utrecht professor that he had lived
in Amsterdam since 1683. Burman's accusation that LeClerc
had abjured his father's religion was countered by LeClerc's
pointing out that his action was an honorable one since he
had acted on the conviction that the Remonstrants had truth
on their side and, by joining them, did not have to dissimulate
nor speak against his conscience. And finally, when Burman
had attacked his scholarship by ridiculing his excessive reliance
on dictionaries, LeClerc had replied that he used not only
dictionaries but also indices.[37]

Burman's *Le Gazettier Menteur, ou Mr. le Clerc convaincu de
Mensonge et de Calomnie* (1710) is a short work filled with
choler and vituperation.[38] After calling LeClerc a "Gallule"
and an outsider, he belittled his knowledge of theology, of
Hebrew, and of the Ancients and topped his remarks by calling
him a liar "who looks for fights" and a "Dictator of the republic
of letters." In *Bibliothèque Choisie* (Tome XX, Part 2, Article
XV, 1710), LeClerc included a notice saying that he was

disengaging from further wrangling with Burman who was stuffed with pride and vanity.

Much has been made of LeClerc's quarrels; in general they led nowhere and were a discredit to the combatants. The arguments were seldom settled because the topics were seldom worth the settling. Along with the Bentley and Burman quarrels, LeClerc was involved in inconclusive exchanges with Vander Waeyen, with Kidder, with Cave, with Graevius, and with Bayle. In most cases LeClerc thought he was defending truth by attacking abuse of the use of reason but he, himself, was capable of deviating from the use of moderation and of reason when he forgot his own precepts by transforming argument into name-calling and awkward irony.

The year 1713 seems to have been a turning point in his life. In that year he gave up *Bibliothèque Choisie*—perhaps he wanted to spend more time as professor of ecclesiastical history; perhaps he was deeply saddened by the death of Van Limborch which had occurred the previous year; perhaps he was worn out by his steady labors and his many skirmishes. Whatever the causes, his output, although sharply diminished, was still impressive. *Bibliothèque Ancienne et Moderne* was started and he was editor. However, much of the material may well have been the work of British correspondents. Other than this work, his main writings included *Histoire des Provinces-Unies des Pays Bas* (1723-28) and a translation and commentary on the Old Testament (1731). These two works were probably completed under extreme pressure. In 1727 he had surrendered his editorship of *Bibliothèque Ancienne et Moderne* and in 1728 had suffered a stroke from which he apparently never fully recovered. But even with waning activity, he had the satisfaction of seeing his earlier works grow in popularity as new editions kept appearing regularly in England and in Holland. He was fully aware that his work was gaining acceptance everywhere in Europe, but most especially in England; he never tired of pointing out that the reprinting of them was tangible proof and reaffirmation of the validity of his discourses and of his arguments.

LeClerc died on January 8, 1736, but popular interest in his writings continued; one need scan only the holdings in the British Museum for evidence. His edition of Grotius's *The Truth of the Christian Religion*, originally published in 1709, was

reprinted at least eight times between 1718 and 1836. In his
lifetime editions had appeared in 1718, 1724, and 1734, with an
English translation in 1711 and six reprintings. *Ars Critica* came
out in at least four editions between 1697 and 1712. There were
three editions (1696, 1714, and 1733) of *The Causes of Incredulity* plus the English translation in 1697.

Recital of some of his works indicates the direction of his
intellectual interests and energies and provides a comprehensive
picture of the problems familiar to the *literati* in England and
in Holland. LeClerc had made it possible for the British and
the Dutch to share each other's thoughts. How valuable he was
to the British may be ascertained by the rapidity with which
his writings were translated; how valuable to the Dutch, by
his lifelong interest in informing them about British thinkers
and their works.

CHAPTER 3

The Bibliothèques

> "Truth, I believe, never runs any risque among
> an enlighten'd People, but when 'tis not permitted
> to be spoken; nor has it any thing to fear from
> Lyes, if suffer'd to encounter them on equal terms:
> So that they, who think they have Truth on their
> side, have nothing to fear from Books, so long as
> they may write, and publish others to defend her."

I *The Milieu*

THE great popularity enjoyed by the periodicals brought
out by Pierre Bayle, Basnage de Beauval, and Jean LeClerc
has been overbalanced by the fact that their works have been
pushed into virtual obscurity by literary historians to whom
journalism was a craft and, very often, a low one. But the
journalist of the late seventeenth and early eighteenth centuries
cannot be completely divorced from other writers during the
period because there was not then such sharp differentiation;
everything that appeared in print belonged in the vast common
field of reading matter. Only as historians have sorted out and
refined the status of these writings has the journalist been
considered a variety of the Grubstreeter and this division has
led to his place among pamphleteers at best or among hack
writers at worst.

To consider Bayle, Basnage, and LeClerc as journalists is not
to depreciate their worth. Even the most casual reader of their
periodicals must be impressed by the learning and the labor
reflected in their writings. Last of three generations of polymaths, they were among the best read and best educated men
of their time. At home in the scholarly world, they were in full
command of what had been written in theology with its long
history of biblical commentary and exegesis; they knew classical
writings and could comment on them with the assurance of

55

long familiarity. In their periodicals is preserved a clear picture of their time. Scholarship is not always obligated to concentrate all its efforts on breaking new ground; clarification of complicated thought or illumination of dark authors are also valuable contributions. Upon such a base these three writers performed needed services for the advancement and strengthening of the republic of letters.

In an age when writers were genre-conscious, they developed their own ways of reporting and knew that clarity and order were central to their reviews and articles. The ability to write cogent abstracts of long, complicated, and often turgidly written books is an art in itself. These journalists, masters of their profession, culled essentials from a book in order to satisfy the needs and interests of readers. When a review consisted mainly of long extracts, they exercised good sense in selecting passages which preserved the core of the book; when there was the urge or the necessity to elaborate, they did so with clarity and force sufficient to invigorate—and, at times, to exasperate—readers. Seldom dull, much more frequently exciting, the journals gave both busy readers and leisurely *literati* material to help keep them abreast of fast-moving intellectual events.

Pierre Bayle has always been credited with having started the vogue for periodicals of review and commentary with his journal *Nouvelles de la République des Lettres*. It appeared initially in 1684 and LeClerc began *Bibliothèque Universelle et Historique* in January, 1686. In 1687 Bayle quit writing his journal and in that same year Basnage de Beauval brought out *Histoire des Ouvrages des Sçavans*, which was a continuation of Bayle's periodical. Essentially all three had the same general purposes: to report on new books; to provide synopses and comments; and to write for a general public outside the limits of the academic world. Yet, with these same basic goals, they produced very different periodicals. Bayle's work reflected his lively, excitable mind, but his skepticism bordering on Pyrrhonism made his journal more provocative than informative. Basnage masked his own personality and wrote objective resumés without much commentary. As a result, his journal was more pedestrian but more informative than was Bayle's. In dealing with British works, both were handicapped by their limited knowledge of English and, therefore, had to depend on translations or on reports from their London correspondents. LeClerc combined the best qualities of both men. An expert in finding the good points in a work as well as in spotting its weaknesses, he presented a journal filled with fresh excitement. His writing was highly organized for the benefit of the reader; he had recognized more fully than had his journalistic contemporaries the need for a system in writing reviews and reports.

Invariably he stated the main points of the book, forestalled hostile criticism, copied solid and substantial extracts and interspersed among them his own comments, always so indicated either in the text or in marginalia. Since he was by nature a man of strong convictions and positive notions, his commentaries leaned heavily toward the didactic and very often toward the dogmatic. When aroused by personal attack or when questioned about the sincerity of his motives, he revealed a rancorous, abrasive, and hostile character boldly seen in his spontaneous and antagonistic reportage. For readers of later generations to whom the hot issues of that day had cooled and even congealed, only the rather disagreeable and discourteous commentaries remain, but for his contemporaries his journalism was always lively and vital in a way which opened opportunities for discussion and for taking sides.

LeClerc had in his favor the ability to read and write English fluently. In a world of polyglots this achievement in itself is not outstanding, but since his colleagues were ill-equipped to deal with the overwhelming mass of material originating in England, the major source of ideas being introduced into the republic of letters, this advantage assumed great importance. Very often, when he discussed British books, he emphasized the value of reading the original texts.

Just as their periodicals have been consigned to the realm of forgotten, neglected or, at best, background material, the journalists themselves have been caught in the caprice of literary history. Historians have been attracted to Bayle, but the magnet was his *Dictionnaire Historique* and not his journal. Basnage de Beauval has been too long ignored and still awaits appraisal. LeClerc, somehow, falls between the fame of Bayle and the obscurity of Basnage. From time to time his work has been examined or used in footnotes, but his importance as an Anglo-Dutch intermediary has suffered because of the emphasis given his disputes, his imbroglios, and his wranglings in which historians have taken an interest incommensurate with their importance.

LeClerc is well worth examination not only on account of his excellent ability as a journalist but also for his longevity in the field of learned reporting. He started early in 1686 and, except for the years between 1691 and 1703, continued without interruption until 1728. As a result, through him is presented a clear, long-range view of Anglo-Dutch cultural relations. The basic nature of the limits he had set on his work was so well defined that the picture is never blurred. Like his mind, his work was always clear in concept and in method. Often, he may be cited for errors or for obtuseness but never for willful obscurity, sham, or vanity.

In *Bibliothèque Universelle et Historique* he clearly stated that he would deal only with contemporary works; in *Bibliothèque Choisie,* he expanded the boundaries to include earlier ones; in *Bibliothèque Ancienne et Moderne* he focused attention on British works, old and new, but deliberately excluded French and Dutch publications. In all three he addressed himself to intelligent readers too busy to read difficult and long books and to serious students in need of competent guidance. As for the truly learned, he contended that they could read and understand the originals.

LeClerc's journals were superior to those of Bayle and Basnage because of his direct contact with the finest minds of his time. They knew many important English writers but LeClerc was more closely associated with them. For example, although both Bayle and LeClerc knew Locke, LeClerc maintained a much closer relationship with him. The same situation applied to Bishop Burnet and to Shaftesbury. In addition, through his other works, especially his editions of classics, LeClerc was much better known at Oxford and, more especially, at Cambridge, where he had good correspondents in Needham, Davies, Wasse, and Barnes, whose names and works have almost been lost in literary history but who were extremely valuable sources of topical information.

The exact measure of LeClerc's success is not hard to determine; the many *aucti-catalogi* of his Dutch contemporaries are a readily available and reliable yardstick. Examination of some of them yields much information on the depth of penetration of his *Bibliothèques.* They existed in complete sets or in partial ones in the holdings of the following: Hubertus Gregorius a Vryhoff (October 21, 1754); Petrum De Hondt (after 1751); Constantijn Huyghens (September 26, 1701); Philip van Limborch (October 4, 1712); Theodorus Janssonius ab Almoloveen (April 25, 1713); Gisbertus Cuperus (August 30, 1717); Theodorus Boendermaker (March 30, 1722); Hermannus van der Wall (September 7, 1734); Pieter Burman (February 27, 1742).[1]

A secondary value of these *aucti-catalogi* is their strong evidence of Dutch interest in British writings in theology, science, and literature. Constantijn Huyghens, Dutch poet and friend of John Donne, had in his library the following: Donne's *Sermons*, Boyle's *Style of the Holy Scriptures*, Quarles's *Divine Poems*, Vaughan's *Sacred Poems*, Ogilby's translation of Virgil, Chaucer's *Works*, Shakespeare's *Plays*, Spenser's *The Faerie Queene*, and others. Herman Boerhaave, the eminent Leyden physician and scientist, had among his books Swift's *A Tale of a Tub* and Garth's *The Dispensary* plus many scientific books. Gosvinus Uilenbroek, bibliophile of Amsterdam, had copies of the plays of Congreve, Rowe's *Jane Shore*, Steele's *The Christian Hero*, and Collier's *A Short View of the English Stage*. In Pieter Burman's library were French translations of *Gulliver's Travels* and *A Tale of a Tub* as well as Steele's *Oeuvres Diverses* and *La Bibliothèque des Dames*. The scholar Anthony van Dale had many English books including the poems of Rochester and of Stephen Duck, the plays of Lee, the works of Addison, eight volumes of *The Spectator* and four of *The Tatler*. English writers included in Reverend Aymon's library were Swift, Pope, Blackmore, Roscommon, and the "best plays, chosen out of all the best authors" in sixteen volumes. The foregoing does not exhaust the roster but indicates a significant readership of English works among Dutch intellectuals.[2]

On the other hand, Dutch works received far less attention in England. Although Burnet, Locke, Temple, Shaftesbury, Addison, and others maintained considerable interest and although translations into English existed in sufficient numbers to indicate passing curiosity in Dutch letters, there was general indifference on the part of the British.

The roles of Bayle, Basnage, and LeClerc as intermediaries were of great importance at this time; they were not pioneers but were capable publicists in the development and in the perpetuation of stronger cultural ties between the two countries.

Between 1684 and 1691 they devoted most of their pages to
British books and, in general, reported on the same ones. According to LeClerc, some readers had complained about the duplica-
tion but, apparently, he could do nothing to remedy the situation.
In spite of the overlapping, there was a large readership and
each journal in its turn prospered.

LeClerc more than Bayle and Basnage saw the journal as a
powerful intellectual tool, valuable for reporting news of what
was being published and for promoting works in harmony with
his own views. He was free to select books for review and
commentary without interference from the publisher, but he
was practical and judicious to include frequent notices that
all books reviewed or mentioned could be purchased from his
bookseller in Amsterdam.

II   Bibliothèque Universelle et Historique

Since LeClerc's contribution to British and Dutch cultural
exchange may be seen by means of a listing of the works he
reviewed and introduced, what follows is, in essence, an annotated catalog of important writings of the time. The roster is
inevitably a long one, but even at the risk of inducing tedium,
it must be recorded in order to establish his importance as an
intermediary.

The scene was very promising when LeClerc started *Bibliothèque Universelle et Historique*. Arrangements had been made
for distribution in London through the bookshop of Sam. Smith
so that the journal could reach readers in England as well as
in Holland. Even Dryden would refer to it in his dedication to
Aeneid. "LeClerc has told us lately, and I believe has made it
out, that David's *Psalms* were written in as arrant rhyme as
they are translated."[3]

It was originally conceived as a collaborative work with
LeClerc shouldering the main responsibility and with Cornard
de la Croze functioning as his assistant. Jacques Bernard and
a network of British and Dutch correspondents supplied much
of the news of what was coming from British and Dutch presses.
With so many people involved directly and indirectly, LeClerc
insisted on a policy of anonymity. It prevailed at the start but,
by the fourth volume, De la Croze, without consultation with
LeClerc, broke the policy and after that, LeClerc allowed

identification of authorship. This breach was the first major problem. Later, after LeClerc had written all of the ninth and tenth volumes, trouble arose again between them in preparation of the eleventh when LeClerc, evidently assuming the authority of a censor, refused to approve some of De la Croze's excerpts which, in LeClerc's opinion, contained dubious judgments. As a result, LeClerc felt obliged to indicate to his readers those articles and excerpts which he, himself, had written and to disclaim responsibility for those by his assistant. This division of their labor needed to be explained because LeClerc's critics too often considered all of this periodical his work and took the liberty to attack him when their fire should have been directed toward De la Croze. After the thirteenth volume, LeClerc assumed full control and wrote all the rest through the nineteenth.[4]

In dealing with this critical confusion, LeClerc cited Marcus Meibom, professor at Amsterdam, Christian Juncker, the Leipzig journalist and Dr. William Cave, Canon of Windsor, who had made wrong attributions. He took full advantage of their mistakes and, in one sharp blow, cut down these critics as well as his assistant. Moralizing, he lectured them, "He, that will censure any one, must take care not to mistake one Man for another, lest the Innocent should suffer for the Guilty."[5]

An overview of *Bibliothèque Universelle et Historique* shows that LeClerc was faithful to his commitment to consider only current publications. Although having some choice, he was necessarily limited by the kinds of books published and by topics of most interest. It is evident that the new thoughts originated mainly in England and that they concentrated heavily on science, philosophy, theology and, to a lesser extent, on philology and classical scholarship. Literature, in general, received scant attention. LeClerc, with a distrust for poetry and allegory, lacked appreciation and knowledge of British poets and sensed that his readers shared his view. Responsive to their tastes, he was, to some extent, instrumental in delaying popular acceptance of English literature, especially its poetry, in Holland.

In the account of his life he said that he had cast aside thoughts of becoming a poet to pursue what he called more urgent and important work. In a trenchant comment on some verses Locke had written as part of the preface to Dr. Sydenham's *De morbus acutis,* LeClerc said that the "Elegaick Verses

of Mr. *Locke*'s . . . are full of Wit and Fancy, but the stile of
them is not altogether exact or Poetical. He had too little esteem
for the Poets to throw away much Time in reading them, and
to take pains to imitate them."[6]

A closer view of the periodical shows how the books he chose
to review or mention paralleled his own interests. A leader
among the Dutch Remonstrants, he dealt with theological books
displaying moderation, reason, and tolerance, but in order to
maintain a good balance, to lend an air of excitement and to
preserve some degree of objectivity, he often included hostile,
critical writings. Exposure of opposing points of view served
him well. He became embroiled in disputes and his journal
became a forum for self-defense.

In general, LeClerc was in the vanguard of contemporary
thought and his journal reflects his position. If *Bibliothèque
Universelle et Historique* did no more than to promote interest
in Locke's work, it would have been sufficient. It was good
enough to make its own way in the republic of letters, but
LeClerc's support accelerated its movement. When Locke's
Method of Indexing a Commonplace Book appeared in a French
translation, LeClerc published a twenty-five page resumé in
the issue for July, 1686. In so doing, he first brought Locke's
name before a large and general Continental readership. A little
later, Locke sent him a manuscript of a short version of *An
Essay Concerning Human Understanding*, which he translated
and printed in the issue for January, 1688. This abridgment
was well received and was soon published independently with
a dedication to the Earl of Pembroke. Although LeClerc said
that it had been printed to satisfy a few of Locke's friends and
to give an idea of its fuller content, he reported with amusement
that some readers believed that he had "Father'd it upon an
English Man, to know what the World thought of it."[7] LeClerc
anticipated the complete work by informing his readers that
Locke would soon bring it out and that it would be available
in Amsterdam. In May, 1690, Locke's completed work was
reviewed in an article of twenty-eight pages. LeClerc provided
a resumé of its thesis regarding innate ideas, pointing out that
its principal purpose was to touch on the whole problem of
distinguishing what is known from what is not.

The issue for December, 1689, contained a review of *A Letter
Concerning Toleration* and the issue for October, 1690, another

review of *A Second Letter Concerning Toleration.* In addition
to reporting on the works themselves and praising Locke for
his brevity, clarity, and vigor, LeClerc attacked the intolerance
he saw in Jonas Proast's arguments against Locke.[8]

The issue for December, 1690, was of special interest because
in it LeClerc printed reviews and comments on Sir Robert
Filmer's *Patriarcha* and Locke's rejoinders, *Two Treatises of
Government* and *An Essay Concerning the true Original Use
of Civil Government.* Reviewing Filmer's work, LeClerc sided
with Locke in attacking the idea favoring absolute monarchy
as a strange doctrine leading to the paradoxical conclusion that
no man is born free and that all are born as slaves to their
prince. By reporting this work in the same volume as Locke's
refutation, LeClerc permitted his readers to see not only Filmer's
basic idea shattered but to see the force of Locke's ideas
enhanced.[9]

Locke's recognition of the worth of *Bibliothèque Universelle
et Historique* went well beyond his interest in its popularizing
his own work. He was an active intermediary in his own right
as in the case of Thomas Sydenham, the best-known physician
of his time. After Locke had received a copy of *Schedula Moni-
toria de Novae Febris Ingressu* (1686), he wrote to Philip van
Limborch on April 10, 1687: "Remember me to M. LeClerc,
and tell him that I have just received . . . a new book of Sydenham's which I have not yet read. If he desires either the book
or a review of it, I will gladly send him either."[10] On this basis it
is highly probable that Locke wrote the article in the issue for
September, 1687. The issue also mentioned three of Sydenham's
lesser works. Locke's personal efforts and LeClerc's collaboration
helped Sydenham's medical ideas gain a strong foothold in
Holland, where Egbertus Veen praised his methods for treatment of chronic diseases and Casper Schelius, who later went
to England, used Sydenham as his "clinical guide." In addition,
Locke's acquaintance with the eminent Dutch physician Lucas
Schacht, professor of medicine at Leyden, brought Sydenham's
work to the attention of Herman Boerhaave, certainly the most
famous and influential doctor and scientist in Holland.

This digressive elaboration testifies to the intricate ways by
which ideas and reputations moved across national boundaries.
Sydenham's place among contemporary physicians in Holland
and in England was more rapidly assured not only by Locke's

interest but by LeClerc's support. Strong personal ties, alert
correspondents, and a community of interest, as herein noted,
show the great value of such a periodical in the movement of
thought throughout the republic of letters.

LeClerc was very much aware of the steady stream of writings
by British scientists and showed his awareness of their importance in the pages of his journal. In the issue of November, 1686,
he reviewed Isaac Barrow's *Euclid's Elements,* mentioned briefly
John Flamsteed's *De Temporis Acquatione Diatriba . . .,* and
reviewed William Molyneux's book on the telescope. The list
of scientific works is especially notable in the general field of
medicine. Here LeClerc reviewed works by Robert Boyle, Walter
Charleton, and Thomas Browne, whose complete works were
announced in the May, 1686, issue.

The greatest contribution which LeClerc made in the field
of scientific achievement was his citation and review of Isaac
Newton's *Philosophiae Naturalis Principia Mathematica.* In
October, 1687, he announced this work and in March, 1688,
printed a fourteen-page review of it. This article is a landmark
in the movement of Newton's work to the Continent. The most
celebrated scientific work of the century had been overlooked
or, at least, had gone unnoticed except by LeClerc. The strong
possibility of Locke's hand in its appearance cannot be ignored.
The review consisted of a careful summary of the general topics
and of a few lengthy excerpts from Book III. LeClerc, realizing
that the subject was outside the area of his competence and
possibly beyond his full understanding, wisely chose to refrain
from commentary. This lack in view of his interest in the new
science may be attributed to his having been unwilling or to
his having been unable to accept general principles or theories
as a foundation for logical argument. His reliance on analysis
rather than on principles is clearly evident in the preface to
Physica, which appeared in 1696.

Thomas Baker, LeClerc's contemporary and adversary, in
commenting on *Physica,* believed that "after all the discoveries
that have been talked of and improvements that have been made
in nature, [LeClerc] has been forced to proceed in an analytical
method for want of principles to go upon."[11] And in modern
times, Lynn Thorndike has followed Baker by saying that
LeClerc "held that general principles could not be found" and,
therefore, advocated "analytical method from particulars."[12]

While his review of *Physica* reflected LeClerc's limitations as
a scientist or as an historiographer of science, his recognition of
its importance was highly visible in his journal and, for this
reason among others, his role as an intermediary in this area
was outstanding.

When LeClerc dealt with theology he was on familiar ground
and provided his readers with exciting accounts of the turbulence
reflected in new books. Bishop Burnet, his long-time friend, was
foremost among theologians represented in *Bibliothèque Universelle et Historique*. With his sharp understanding of the value
of wide circulation through this journal, Burnet most likely served
as his own intermediary and since his strong emphasis on
Protestantism and tolerance appealed to LeClerc, his ideas
invariably received strong support. In the issue for April, 1686,
there appeared a very brief statement on his *The History of
the Reformation of the Church of England.* LeClerc pointed
out that this work was so popular that it had been translated
into Latin by Melchior Mittelhorzerus and into French by
M. de Rosemond. The latter was reviewed in June, 1687, and
LeClerc observed that Burnet's book was now too well known
to need a resumé; he simply praised the orderly, authoritative
handling of the subject, the insistence on facts and the citation
from reliable sources.

The Burnet-Varillas controversy flourished in the journal.[13]
Burnet had attacked Varillas for his excessive use of conjecture
and groundless notions and had cited fifty-two instances where
he believed Varillas had been in error. When Varillas replied
to Burnet, LeClerc reviewed the rejoinder in the issue for
November, 1687, dismissing Varillas as a dealer in fiction. Later,
Burnet kept the controversy alive by challenging Varillas to
produce some of the manuscripts he had cited in his *History
of Heresy.* In reporting their heated exchange, LeClerc praised
Burnet for exposing Varillas's fictional history and, at the same
time, warned Varillas either to maintain "un silence éternel"
or to produce "quelque chose de semblable."

LeClerc cited Bishop Burnet's *An Abridgement of the Prerogatives of S. Ann...* in which he had argued that monks
had forged genealogies and had mentioned nonexistent works.
This review was based on William Clagett's English translation
and appeared in the issue for October, 1688. The December,
1688, issue praised Burnet for his sympathy for the plight of

the French Protestants as expressed in *The Letter writ by the last assembly of the Clergy of France* and mentioned the treatise *Examen des Raisons de Parker contre le Test* as a work very well known in the Dutch provinces. Among Burnet's other writings noted were *The Life of William Bedell, Bishop of Kilmore in Ireland* (1685) and *The Life and Death of Sir Matthew Hale* (1682).[14] Just as LeClerc had praised Locke for his concise and clear style and for his eminent good sense, so he lauded Bishop Burnet. Years later he would remember with pleasure Burnet's "beautiful Strokes of Wisdom, Penetration, Caution, Modesty and Sincerity."[15]

Although LeClerc's reporting of theological works was so extensive as to appear diffuse, he made it a point to direct his readership toward divines whose works presented ideas and points of view in line with his own. For example, he chose to examine the works of William Clagett, the close friend of Burnet.[16] From May, 1686, through December, 1688, LeClerc printed citations and brief reviews of his writings, all of which were either attacks on the Church of Rome or strong theological arguments against superstition. Another relevant example is John Lightfoot, whose biblical studies paralleled LeClerc's interests. Accordingly, in the issue for April, 1686, he devoted fifty-two pages to *Opera Omnia*. Edward Stillingfleet, the latitudinarian, was also well represented. His works were mentioned and reviewed in issues from January, 1686, to November, 1689. Here again LeClerc presented works designed to rout idolatry and to fortify the independence of the Church of England. Other British theologians prominently mentioned were Archbishop William Wake, Archbishop John Tillotson, Archbishop James Ussher, and Henry Dodwell. Of these, LeClerc had highest esteem for Tillotson and Dodwell. After Tillotson's death, LeClerc wrote a defense of his writings, characterizing him as "a Man excellent for a clear Head, great Penetration, exquisite Reasoning, profound Knowledge of true Divinity, and solid Piety, for a peculiar Plainness and Elegance of Stile without any Affectation...."[17] He called Henry Dodwell "a Learned Gentleman, of great penetration and skill in Ecclesiastical Antiquities" and added a personal appraisal to the effect that "No man has a greater value for his Writings than myself, and I have frequently made honorable mention of him...; tho' in some points I dissent from him."[18]

There were two unusual items. He announced the availability
in Amsterdam "chez the Veuve Swart" of *Enquiry into the
Physical and Literal Sense* ... by Reverend Charles Morton of
Charlestown, Massachusetts, which had just been published in
London in 1687, and William Penn's *Zonder Cruis geen Kroon*
(*No Cross, No Crown*), which had been translated into Dutch
by Willem Sewel in 1687. Here Penn is identified not for his
place among Quakers but for his position as "Gouverneur et
Propriétaire de la Pennsylvanie." Thus LeClerc may have been
a pioneer in introducing American works to the Continent.[19]

LeClerc's overwhelming interest in British thought dominated
Bibliothèque Universelle et Historique. As a result, it is a rich
treasury of contemporary review and critical commentary on
many works which had been buried immediately after their
topicality had waned as well as of works destined to have
memorable lives reaching far beyond the time of the republic
of letters. The contents of the periodical leave no doubt that
intelligent readers in both England and in Holland looked for
instruction more than for pleasure in their reading matter. The
lack of reporting *belles-lettres* until about 1691 may be disap-
pointing but has negative value because it emphasizes the high
premium placed on topical expression and on controversial
writings. On the other hand, it is inviting to speculate that had
LeClerc or his correspondents detected among readers an interest
in British literature, might he have yielded to include such
material? His was not an isolated case. A check of Bayle's and
Basnage's periodicals up to 1691 reveals a relatively similar
situation. However, between 1691 and 1703 there was steadily
mounting interest as indicated in Basnage's journal. But in 1691
LeClerc had quit his periodical not to return to journalism until
1703, and when he resumed this writing he too realized the
necessity to cater to this neglected area.

III   Bibliothèque Choisie

By the time LeClerc was persuaded to undertake the second
journal, *Bibliothèque Choisie,* he had become well known
throughout England and Holland as a controversialist in theology, in historiography, and in biblical commentary. In England
his work was receiving increased attention as a result of the
translations which had appeared almost immediately after the

original Amsterdam editions. These translations during the years
when he was free from editorship clearly indicate the depth
of his penetration into the intellectual world of London. Further
help in promoting his reputation came from Basnage de Beauval,
who included frequent mention of LeClerc's work in his journal.
For example, Basnage reviewed LeClerc's corrected version of
the sixth edition of Moreri's *Dictionnaire Historique* in the issue
for July, 1691, praising LeClerc for purging the original of many
errors. He reviewed *Parrhasiana* in the May, 1699, issue and
noted that commentary was unnecessary because "M. LeClerc
est assez célèbre dans la République des Lettres." In his review
of the French translation of Arthur Bury's *The Naked Gospel*
in May, 1691, Basnage pointed out that it was simply a reworking
of LeClerc's account of the life of Eusebius, which had already
appeared in *Bibliothèque Universelle et Historique*.

LeClerc's ever-widening popularity was reflected in *Bibliothèque Choisie*. When compared with the first journal, it is
distinguished by more boldness, more authority, more liveliness,
and wider range. Its whole tone was influenced by a different
handling of the material. LeClerc abandoned the restrictive
form of reviewing and adopted the flexible one of the essay
and miscellany and, in this way, was in a favorable position
to include his own commentary more freely and to indulge in
digressions very often for the express purpose of engaging his
adversaries in battle. In *Bibliothèque Universelle et Historique*
he had established himself as an outspoken reviewer and commentator and had made his reputation as an exciting disputant
and controversialist. Now he continued to encourage such activity
and presented a periodical which often was a veritable battle
ground not only for him but for his audience. From the very
beginning he invited controversy. With mild irony he said in
the prefatory remarks to the first issue, "I have no idea of
quarreling with anyone. There are some people in the world
who are envious and pick fights. I won't give them the satisfaction
of a quarrel, which is what they itch for." In the preface to
the second tome he announced that he had already been maligned.
The main complaint was that he did not deal enough with
new books. He contended that a book which the reader had
never read is for him a new one and that there are old books
which are new and new ones which are old. In the preface
to the third issue he defended himself against a troublesome,

picayune critic who had found an error of fact in the previous issue. LeClerc had been assailed for attributing a medal to the "petit-fils" of Drusius when it should have been the "fils." To such a critic he replied that he made mistakes occasionally and taunted him by saying that if critics worked on the same subjects as he did, they would excel him because of all the erudition and exactitude of which only they were capable.

In the preface to Tome V (1705) he observed that it came out while Europe was at war and that he hoped for an early peace. But he said that his main interest was concern for another kind of republic—the republic of letters. While he talked of military peace he said that he was girding himself for intellectual war, having become entangled in controversies with the Bishop of Meaux, the Jesuit Father Despineuil, and, especially, with the Benedictine monk, Father Martianay. He hoped that places where men might speak their minds would continue to exist— evidently a sharp rebuke to Paris, where the intellectual atmosphere precluded the freedom which he was enjoying in Amsterdam. His zest for battle grew. In the preface to Tome XII (1707) he called attention to his quarrel with Pierre Bayle and asked the readers' indulgence; he said he would not mention the controversy again. The reason was obvious. Bayle had died on December 28, 1706, and in remarks, evidently written earlier, LeClerc had accused him of belonging to the Republic of Atheists.

A more important and enduring difference between the first and second periodical is in their contents. In *Bibliothèque Universelle et Historique* there had been a dearth of reviews dealing with classical scholarship and with literary works; in *Bibliothèque Choisie* this gap was adequately filled. There were two reasons for inclusion of news on these subjects. In the first place, LeClerc had become increasingly involved as an editor and as an explicator of the classics; in the second, as has been noted, he had recognized the quickening pace of interest in British literature in Basnage's periodical during the years when he, himself, had been out of journalistic work.

In classical scholarship Basnage had kept Continental interest alive in the Bentley-Boyle dispute over the Phalaris Letters by reviewing Bentley's attack in the April, 1698, issue and, in the June issue for that year he had cited Boyle's reply. Barnes's edition of Euripides and Creech's edition of Lucretius were

mentioned, but of more interest, perhaps, were the notices of
Dryden's translations of Virgil's *Georgics* and of the life of
Polybius. Basnage called Dryden "... un des meilleurs poètes
d'Angleterre."

In dealing with literary writings, Basnage's correspondents
had brought attention to Dryden's *Love Triumphant, The Mock
Astrologer,* and *Oedipus,* and had identified their author as
"un de nos plus fameux poètes." Of major interest was the review
in the issue of February, 1699, of Milton's work in general and
mention of *Paradise Lost* and *Paradise Regained.* Even literary
critical works had received some special notice. In May, 1698,
Basnage had reviewed Jeremy Collier's *A Short View of Im-
morality on the Stage* and, two months later, had cited John
Dennis's *The Usefulness of the Stage.* Thomas Rymer's *A Short
View of Tragedy* had been mentioned in the issue for February,
1693, and William Wotton's dissertation on the Ancients and
the Moderns in the issue for November, 1694. In issues before
1703, Basnage had mentioned Thomas Pope Blount's *Remarks
on Poetry,* Richard Blackmore's *Prince Arthur,* Charles Hopkins's
The Art of Love, Roger L'Estrange's *Aesop's Fables,* Matthew
Prior's *Secular Song,* and Sir John Vanbrugh's *The Provok'd Wife.*

As for LeClerc, he predicted that those who knew the temper
and the determination of the British could look forward to
their contributions to the republic of letters. In Tome III, 1704,
in defense of his Anglomania, he had said that if any complain
that he overpraised the British, he must answer that it was the
least recompense which was their due for bringing out excellent
editions of Greek and Latin authors. In other areas he popularized
works destined to become staples in British intellectual history.
He sparked Continental curiosity in the writings of Shaftesbury
and Addison; he insured continuous interest in the new editions
of Locke's work. In theology, he concentrated heavily on Ralph
Cudworth's *The True Intellectual System* and on his own edition
of the works of Erasmus; in science, he cited the works of
George Berkeley and Isaac Newton; and, in history, he reported
in great detail on Clarendon's *History* and on Rymer's *Foedera.*
He dealt with fewer works than he had in the first journal and
in this way was able to report in detail and to remedy the flaw
of excessive diffusion.

LeClerc's precise resumés and clear commentaries appealed
to British readers, and almost simultaneously with the appearance

of an issue of *Bibliothèque Choisie* there came out English
translations in pamphlet form of those articles the booksellers
were sure would sell. Here then is a situation in which English
works, apparently little read but widely known at home, were
put into abbreviated form in French and then translated back
into clear, simple English. LeClerc may well be considered as
having been a popularizer of British works for British readers
as well as a cosmopolitan Dutch intermediary.

IV *Classical Scholarship*

A good judge of classical scholarship, LeClerc had been impressed by British editors and warmly supported the work of
the new generation of scholars among whom he singled out
Barnes, Needham, Wasse, and Davies for special commendation.
Without exception, their new editions indicated to him that the
British were, at last, generating scholarly writings to rival the
Dutch ones. Part of his enthusiasm grew out of his own activity
in this field. To make sure that his readership would recognize
his competence as critic and judge of classical scholarship, he
reported at length in the first issue of *Bibliothèque Choisie* on
a new edition of *Elegiae* by Albinovanus, which had been
brought out under joint editorship, one of whose members was
he, using the pseudonym Theodore Gorallus.

In the article LeClerc noted the three standards required
to judge the Ancients properly: The critic must determine the
accuracy of the new text by comparing it with extant original
manuscripts; he must explicate obscure passages using Lipsius's
methodology as the touchstone; and he must take into account
orderly presentation of commentary and avoid needless digression. In a general statement he warned editors against imitating
predecessors who had been so prolix that they had explicated
equally what was clear and what was obscure. He said that
faulty scholarship often arose from amassing infinite examples
of parallel passages even when such comparison was useless
for clarification of text. He added that such enterprise grew out
of vanity and clogged commentaries with senseless and extra-
neous material.

Having laid down principles and exposed some hazards, he
undertook a systematic report of new British scholarship. In
Tome III he devoted a complete article to Latin poetry newly

edited in England and, to forestall Continental critics envious, perhaps, of British editors, said that it was his duty to report excellence whatever its source and, therefore, he could not overlook the British even though some might think he was overpraising them. He also acknowledged that much of his news of recently published classical editions came from excellent British correspondents who were privy to what was of concern and interest to readers in Protestant countries.

After this preface, he reviewed the new edition of Horace by "Les Directeurs de l'Académie de Cambridge," which had been printed in 1696 by Jacob Tonson. The article also mentioned new editions of Terence (1701), Virgil (1701), and Catullus (1702), whose editors were identified only as Cambridge scholars. The entire review was a most favorable one; the editors had done well because, in general, they had followed LeClerc's rules.

Having written on British scholars, he balanced his material by reporting in Tome IV on new Dutch editions of Latin poets. Here, his praise paralleled that which he had bestowed on the British, but in this article he named the editors and the praise was more effective. The new editions included Pieter Burman's *Phaedri* (1698); David Hoogstraat's fifth book of *Fabulorum Aesopiarum* (1701); a complete edition of *Aesop's Fables* (1703) by Frederic Gronovius, Jacobus Gronovius, and Nicholas Dispontyn; Pieter Burman's re-editing of Janus Rutgers's earlier edition of Horace (1699); and Jan Broekhuyzen's edition of the fourth book of Propertius (1702). LeClerc made special mention of the work of Burman and, even more, of Broekhuyzen's. He characterized the latter as being "célèbre par de très-élégants Poësies Latines" and, although the edition had appeared anonymously, LeClerc was so elated with it that he revealed the editor's name.

This program of reviewing classical scholarship now moved from consideration of Roman writers to Greek ones. In Tome VI he cited for special commendation Barnes's edition of Euripides (1694); Nicholas Sudor's edition of Pindar (1697) on which West and Welsted had worked; John Potter's edition of Lycophron (1702); Andrew Papit's edition of Dionysius (1697); and an anonymous edition of Theocritus (1699). Part of LeClerc's purpose in presenting a roster of relatively old editions was for the very practical reason that he wished to

inform his readers of their availability at Henri Schelte's book-
store in Amsterdam.

In Tome XI LeClerc continued this campaign by devoting
a long, laudatory article to John Davies's new edition of Caesar
which had appeared in 1706. He predicted that Davies would
go far if he kept up the good work shown in this edition and
that all British classical scholarship would flourish if the great
progress of recent years were maintained. What had impressed
him most about British scholars was implied in his statement,
"it is necessary not only to copy the style of the Classical
writers, it is more important to understand them and to be
able to think well about them and even to surpass the Ancients
in thinking." Apparently he had found these admirable qualities
in the British.

In the same tome but in a separate article, he dealt with
William Piers's edition of Euripides's tragedies (1703) and considered briefly the problem of translation. He reiterated his
remarks on the difficulty of making good translations, especially
of poetry, and advocated the use of paraphrase if the general
sense was to be captured. Here again he praised Davies for
the excellence of his commentary on Daniel Heinsius's edition
of Maximus Tyrius. He noted Barnes's edition of Anacreon
and then, unaccountably, added citation of and praise for J. H.
Lederling, professor at Strasbourg, for his edition of Homer,
calling it a "translation habile dans la langue Grec."

In subsequent tomes of *Bibliothèque Choisie*, British and
Dutch scholarship continued to receive careful and frequent
treatment. In Tome XV LeClerc announced Kuster's new edition
of Aristophanes and his well-known one of Suidas and, in
another article in this tome, wrote a brief eulogy for Broekhuyzen.

Two Dutch works providing the basis for a single article in
Tome XVI were Michael Rossal's disquisition on Epictetus
and Tiberius Hemsterhuis's version of the *Dialogues* of Lucian.
Of the former LeClerc said that the argument against Epictetus's
being a Christian made good sense; of the latter he commended
the scholarship in textual correction. In a rare notice of scholarly
activity in Germany, he included in Tome XVII mention of
receipt of a letter written in Berlin on November 10, 1708,
by J. Barbeyrac, outlining a project for an edition of Lucretius.

In Tome XIX, LeClerc wrote a long, bitter article in self-
defense against Burman's attack in the preface to the edition

of Petronius Arbiter. He complained that Burman "a vomi des torrens de bile contre moi, dans son Petrone," and that Broekhuyzen and Burman had joined forces against him. Of his relationship with Broekhuyzen, LeClerc recalled having met him but three times in twenty-four years and that on two of those occasions he had been accompanied by a guest.

In Tome XX he mentioned Davies again, not so much to comment on his new edition of Cicero as to cite Richard Bentley's emendations contained in it. A new, abbreviated edition of Longinus's *On The Sublime* in 1710, which was reviewed in Tome XXI, gave LeClerc an opportunity to comment on works designed for students. Although he was aware of an earlier annotated edition which had been published in Utrecht in 1694 as well as of French versions by Boileau and by Dacier, he said that this newer one served a useful purpose. He explained that it was needed since young Englishmen no longer read Longinus because of its scarcity and because of excessive length of commentary in other editions. This more convenient one might encourage study unencumbered by useless editorial material.

LeClerc, who maintained a close relationship with Cambridge scholars, was always ready to help them. He wrote a preface for Wasse's edition of Sallust (1710) and, in Tome XXI, said that in his opinion, it was the best and most accurate one to date. He also announced that Wasse had completed an edition of Diodorus and that an enterprising bookseller ought to publish it.

Succeeding tomes of *Bibliothèque Choisie* continued to present news of activity among Cambridge scholars. Tome XXII contained a laudatory notice of Barnes's edition of the *Iliad* and of the *Odyssey* (1711); Tome XXV reported on Peter Needham's new edition with notes on Isaac Casaubon's older one of Theophrastus's *Characters*. LeClerc commended Needham's avoidance of idle conjecture. Once, said LeClerc, he had had the idea of bringing out an edition of Theophrastus for young scholars, but after reading Needham's he yielded with pleasure. The two had exchanged letters on scholarly matters and some of their correspondence had dealt with this edition. Needham had asked for help and for any notes which LeClerc might be willing to supply, and when LeClerc turned over his notes, Needham had acknowledged the generosity. Then, evidently in reply to a letter from LeClerc about the attacks leveled against his edition of Menander, Needham had written on July 9, 1710, "I can give you no manner of intelligence about the animadversions upon your Menander, which you suspect came from this [Cambridge] university."[20]

Tome XXVI is well known for LeClerc's belated review of Bentley's edition of Horace (1713). The fair and gracious commentary, in the light of their earlier disputes, indicated his recognition of Bentley's superiority.

LeClerc's steady attention to British scholarship and his approval and praise of the newer editors did much to accelerate their importation on a major scale into Holland. By attracting new Dutch readers, he performed a valuable service on behalf of the republic of letters. But emphasis on the British was not at the expense of the Dutch, whose excellence had been so well established that it did not require elaboration. His heavy concentration on the British seems to indicate a reversal or shift of the current which had, heretofore, moved forcefully from Holland.

LeClerc probably had another strong motive for his long, steady reporting of British editions. He had noted a decline in humanity learning and had wanted to do whatever was in his power to remove the decay which he foresaw could lead to the inevitable death of classical scholarship. In *Parrhasiana*, as will be noted in the next chapter, he had already sounded the warning. He knew that sloppy scholarship, pompous erudition, masked ignorance, and sheer vanity were the destroyers. To help cure the disease, he not only established guidelines for critical evaluation of scholarship but supported them with many concrete examples. His great hope seemed to have been that he would provide at least a partial remedy in *Bibliothèque Choisie*. He was convinced that a more effective use of reason could produce a latter-day Grotius and that increased knowledge of the arts could stimulate the Moderns to rival the Ancients. Therefore, he looked to the newer breed of British scholars in the hope that they would emulate and even surpass the great Scaliger.

LeClerc was not the only one to warn of the decay in learning. From a very different point of view Swift, in *A Tale of a Tub*, generally agreed and Pope's utter despair in *The Dunciad* recorded the death of scholarship and the triumph of dullness.

LeClerc, writing well before Pope, had refused to accept defeat which Pope considered inevitable.

> Lo! thy dread Empire, CHAOS! is restored;
> Light dies before thy uncreating word;
> Thy hand, great Anarch! lets the curtain fall;
> And universal Darkness buries All.

V *Theological Works*

British theologians, philosophers, and divines had long been entrenched among the leading citizenry of the republic of letters. An active churchman, LeClerc had taken great interest in writings on theology in *Bibliothèque Universelle et Historique* and his interest became intensified in *Bibliothèque Choisie*. His strong Arminian and latitudinarian convictions as well as his long, personal ties with British leaders whose thinking generally coincided with his own, made him an ideal intermediary. Thoroughly at home among theologians advocating the use of reason, tolerance, and moderation, he reported on and personally participated in endless controversies and his work took on a more exciting but less objective attitude than was the case when he dealt with classical scholarship. Now his periodical was a battlefield upon which he engaged in the hard and bitter fighting for the triumph of truth over superstition and bigotry. He supported Cudworth, Locke, Burnet, and Tindal along with many lesser-known allies. He was no longer an objective journalist because he was convinced that neutrality was really moral disengagement; he valued truth more and, as a result, his contributions were highly subjective. The journal became a chronicle of contemporary theological encounters and after the battles had subsided but had never been concluded, there remained only the valuable residue of his admiration for Locke, his respect for Burnet, and his appreciation for Cudworth.

From the very first issue he threw his full weight behind Cudworth's *The True Intellectual System,* which had been published originally in 1678. LeClerc's reason for renewing interest in this work was that its support of Christian Platonism and its refutation of Hobbesism were now more relevant than they had been. Encouraged by Van Limborch, he set out to revive a work once well known but now a rarity and used

Cudworth's arguments as a strong defense against atheism. His purpose was to cut the ground from under atheistic tendencies by refuting the Hylozoick atheists, especially those in Holland, and to support Cudworth's idea of plastic nature.[21] He condensed the book into a series of abstracts and comments and published them over a period of three years (1703-1706) in seven of the first nine tomes. Some of the articles were extremely lengthy. For example, in Tome III, he devoted almost a hundred pages to the fourth chapter alone, which had considered the question of whether or not the most enlightened pagans believed in a Supreme Being.

In the summary of *The True Intellectual System*, LeClerc recalled Bayle's *Continuation of Various Thoughts concerning Comets*, in which Cudworth had been accused of "Ignorance in the Way of Reasoning" and he, himself, had been labeled an ignoramus. Since Bayle knew very little English, LeClerc heightened the attack against him by pointing out that Cudworth's book needed to be read in the original because a good French translation was almost impossible. "Ceux qui connoissent le génie de la Langue Angloise, et la liberté extraordinaire qui se donnent les Auteurs Anglois à se servir de nouvelles experiences et de figures hardies et même violentes en conviendront facilement."

Modern interest focuses on the Bayle-LeClerc dispute rather than on Cudworth's work. No doubt battle between prominent citizens in the republic of letters enlivened LeClerc's review and provided fresh interest but, in actuality, the essential differences between the thinking of Bayle and LeClerc were minute. Acrimony had so magnified the dispute that it eventually degenerated into name-calling unworthy of both. These were men dedicated to the quest for truth but they traveled different paths. Bayle took the road of the skeptic unwilling to follow reason or philosophy to its very end; LeClerc went along the highway wherever reason led, hoping to reach the point where truth would be self-evident.[22]

The battle has been well chronicled by Rosalie L. Colie, who while sympathetic to Cudworth and LeClerc in presenting and in popularizing their theological ideas, gave the laurel to Bayle as a debater. "Altogether, Bayle handled LeClerc masterfully. Politely, ironically, he responded to each extract as it was issued, chilling LeClerc's ardour with the cool rain of his reason."[23] As for LeClerc, she felt that he was less urbane

but, in heavy-handed fashion, had responded with a mastery
of invective and of memorable sneer. His remarks on Bayle
gave support to her conclusion. In the account of his life, he
had included a sketch of Bayle which was a masterpiece of
irresponsible generality and hot-headed vindictiveness which
he had so often deplored in others. After characterizing him
"a vehement Patron of bad Causes," he wrote:

He was indeed a Man of Eloquence, and one who by a multitude
of Select Words, and a Facetiousness in Things of a serious Nature,
could gain upon the People; not on those, who are pleas'd with
sound Reason, rather than the tickling Charms of empty Harangues.
In Matters of Divinity he was an utter Stranger, and knew nothing
in a manner, but what he heard from Sermons, or had taken from
French Authors; he challeng'd all Divines, and affirm'd that no
Christian School whatsoever, was able to answer the Objections
of the *Manichees,* that is of his own, for he found them out. Now,
were all the true Lovers of the Christian Religion, grievously offended
at the Boaster; for it was plain, that he was a Derider of Religion;
wherefore Mr. LE CLERC thought it proper to deal with him more
clearly and openly, by which it grew to such a height, that when
BAYLE found himself pinch'd home, he endeavour'd all he could
to render his Adversary odious, and like a true Sophister, oppos'd
him with all kind of Railing to his very Death, and left his
opprobrious Writings to be publish'd after it.[24]

Despite the Bayle-LeClerc battle, Cudworth's *The True
Intellectual System* enjoyed a strong revival. Thomas Wise
in an edited abridgment in 1706 weighed the merits of their
arguments and came out in favor of LeClerc. Following an
examination of *Bibliothèque Choisie,* he had concluded that
LeClerc's abstracts had been "faithfully enough done, and the
Original not misrepresented."[25] He disapproved of Bayle for
his habit of digression, chided him for his ignorance of English
and advised him to "level his Darts with an exacter aim than
he did before, to let that Work [Cudworth's] alone."[26]

Any impression that this controversy dominated news of
British theology in the periodical must be tempered by the fact
that throughout the decade of its publication, it was filled with
commentary and abstracts of many other theological writings.[27]
Burnet, Tillotson, Kidder, Whitby, and Tindal were among those
frequently mentioned, discussed, and reviewed.

A less celebrated but more vital battle than the one over

Cudworth was aired in *Bibliothèque Choisie.* Fought by theologians generally of a minor rank, this one touched on very
practical and sensitive points in the matter of the relationship
of Church and State. Abstraction and speculation as had been
encountered in the Cudworth controversy gave way to more
concrete, mundane considerations. Still unsettled and in the
debating stage were the issues dealing with the source of church
authority, the relationship of Church and State and the rights
of the Church and of the people. These points needed discussion and LeClerc provided the forum. In the review of *The
Rights of The Christian Church Asserted,* published anonymously
in 1706, he argued on behalf of basic ideas in harmony with
his own beliefs which were not yet fully acceptable to the
traditionally-minded in Holland and in England. Just as he
could not possibly have seen how far-reaching would be his
involvement with Bayle over Cudworth's book, so he could
not possibly have envisioned the fervor, excitement, and serious
debate this new book would call forth.

LeClerc's article won instantaneous popularity and immediately
after publication in 1707, was translated into English and was
published in 1708 as a separate pamphlet with a prefatory letter
addressed to "a Noble Peer."[28] The unidentified Lord had asked
the anonymous writer of the preface for his opinion of this
review. After noting that it fully answered his "Expectation
from a Man of Mr. LeClerc's known Abilitys [*sic*]" (p. iii), he
observed the irony in LeClerc's function as an intermediary
when he said, "Your Lordship perhaps will smile, when I tell
you, that I think this Account in French, tho of an English
Book, ought to be translated back again into English: For I
do not expect to see a better Extract of it by any English Hand,
unless the Author himself would undertake it..." (p. iii). He
acknowledged LeClerc's worth as a publicist by adding, "I
believe many will be prevail'd upon to consider the Arguments,
when they see 'em in a less compass, who will not, thro the
Prejudice they have conceiv'd against the Book it self, be
otherwise rightly appriz'd of 'em" (p. iii). He called LeClerc
"a Learned and Ingenious Foreigner" whose article had provoked
"both the greatest Reception, and the most violent Opposition, of any Book we have had printed among us for many
years" (p. iv).

LeClerc realized that a foreigner's intrusion into British affairs

might embitter some readers and he tried to placate them with
a full statement of his high regard and respect for the Church
of England, "which is too much enlighten'd, and too wise, to
carry things to such Extremitys [sic] ... that she meant to depend
in divers respects on the Sovereign Authority of King and
Parliament."²⁹ Forthrightly, he acknowledged his awkward position as an outsider and explained as well as he could that he
did not "mean to take any part in the particular Disputes, which
the Learned in *England* have among themselves about the Independent Power of Bishops; and much less to reflect in any sort
on the Church of *England*" (p. 2). He described it "the most
Illustrious of all the Protestant Churches; which abounds with
Learned Men, and a Multitude of Books full of good Sense,
Learning, and Piety" (pp. 2-3). Still concerned with possible
hostility, he protected himself by stating that he had no personal
knowledge of the author of the book he had reviewed, had
no "concern with him" and had "no particular Interest to defend
him" (p. 3). He completed the overcautious defense by lauding
the whole British nation which "has too much Light and good
Sense to be abus'd by false Reasonings, especially when 'tis
lawful ... to oppose them with better" (p. 3). Hopefully, having
established a firm, amicable, and detailed foundation acceptable
to statesmen and churchmen, he was now free to deal with
the controversial volume.

Essentially *The Rights* had two purposes: to show the extent
of sovereign power—how men live "in the Liberty of the State
of Nature," depending only on God and "their own Consciences;
and to examine the proofs drawn from reason and Scripture"
by which churchmen had established their independent power.
The author argued strongly in favor of the first and vehemently
against the second. Support of the ascendancy of sovereign over
churchly power culminated in his insistence that the idea of
their being independent was absurd because the ruler "annexes
Preferments and other Advantages to the Teachers of his own
Religion, exclusive of all others" (p. 24) and, as a result, the
clergy become the ruler's deputies. From this undeniable situation
it was inevitable and even self-evident that the sovereign power,
i.e., the State, was supreme. Carrying his argument a step
further, he insisted that if, indeed, the Church was as independent
as some believed—that it could make its own laws in matters
of faith, that it could determine what the people should believe,

that it could punish those unwilling to accept arbitrary decisions without violation of freedom of conscience—it must follow that the clergy's "Authority is the most Absolute, the most Arbitrary, the most Unlimited, and the most Unaccountable of any among Men" (p. 27). Furthermore, he said that with such great power, churchmen could never be called "to account for their Male-Administration [sic]" (p. 27). He attacked the generally accepted tenet that the Church formed a "particular and Independent Government" by saying that if it were so, the Church could make its own laws, execute them, and even transmit its power to its successors. Yet, such power was a fiction. Ever since the days of Henry VIII, the clergy had had no such dominion "without the Order and express Consent of King and Parliament, without which nothing can have the Force of a Law in *England*" (p. 30). This argument was so intense that it shook the very foundations of a basic principle among many divines, especially High Churchmen.

LeClerc was not surprised at the vehement opposition to the book among some of the clergy. Although its author had attacked "with all his might the Pretensions of such as are call'd High Churchmen," LeClerc appealed for toleration and calmness, insisting that wise and moderate members of the Church of England appreciated that their Church could withstand any attack. The review took the usual form of extracts followed by comments, identified as such in marginal notations. He pointed out that the author had in mind not the present Establishment but only those whose pretensions were contrary to British laws and to the authority of King and Parliament. In order to emphasize the author's position and to excite curiosity so that laymen would read the original, he copied long extracts from the introduction. Then he said he was embarrassed for lack of space not to have done more for the rest of the book and simply listed the ten chapter headings which elaborated on the points which had been mentioned in the introduction. Among the more vital were: "that there cannot be two Independent Powers in the same Society" (p. 28); that the Clergy's belief it has "a Right to exclude People from the Church of Christ" (p. 28) is absurd; that the insistence of independent power "prevents the further spreading of the Gospel" (p. 28) and is "destructive to the Interest of Religion, and is the cause of those corruptions under which Christianity labours" (p. 28).

LeClerc attacked Bayle's well-known claim "That Religion is not necessary to Society, and that a Commonwealth of Atheists might as well subsist, as the very best among the antient [sic] Pagans" (p. 11). He argued that the Sovereign had no right to determine for the people what was true or false in matters of religion and insisted that exercise of reason was essential when changes were made in government. "People ought to examine what [the clergy] are doing, lest [the people] fall from a lesser Ill into a greater, which often happens" (p. 24). In the concluding remark, he said that this was the best book he had read on the subject and commended it for having "much Force and fine Reasoning" and as for opponents, they ought not to feel abused but now had an opportunity to refute the arguments.

Refutations, arguments, and vitriolics came fast. Of chief interest is the fact that before the article in *Bibliothèque Choisie* had been translated into English, most clergymen had been silent. Therefore, when they lashed out, it was not against *The Rights* but against LeClerc's abstract and judgment. Here, then, is a prime example of his power as an intermediary and as a popularizer of current thought.

From the many hostile pamphlets LeClerc chose six representative ones which he consolidated into an article in Tome XXI (1711). But before undertaking his defense, he reminded readers of his impartiality and of his periodical's being neutral ground where all had the right to be heard. Ironically, he said that he did not judge books which appear in *Bibliothèque Choisie* "except for [himself], and in the Secresy [sic] of [his] own Closet" (p. 2). Indeed, he insisted, "Je n'ai aucun droit de dire en public tout ce que je pense de chacun, soit en bien, soit en mal" and closed his prefatory remarks with the assertion, "Je parlerai de ces refutations, sans m'engager en aucune manière dans cette dispute."

His defense was of such general interest that it was translated almost immediately into English and published in London as *The Rights of the Christian Church Adjusted: Being the Extract and Judgment of Mr. LE CLERC upon those AUTHORS who have Written against [The Book Intitul'd] The Rights of the Christian Church Asserted &c, viz. Dr. HICKES, Dr. TURNER, Mr. WOTTON, Mr. HILL, Mr. CAROL, Mr. OLDSWORTH &c....1711.*

LeClerc dealt first with George Hickes, the most vehement

of the opponents. In 1709, Hickes had written a preface in the form of a letter addressed to the anonymous translator of *An Answer to Mr. de Fontenelle's History of Oracles . . . with Some Reflections upon the Remarks of Mr. Le Clerc, in his Bibliothèque Choisie* and had described LeClerc as "one of the greatest Latitudinarians, that this wicked age of free-thinkers, . . . free-writers, [and] . . . free-livers, hath any where produced." The translator, fortified by Hickes's letter, had added his own satire of LeClerc as "a pleasant Man, [who] loves a Farce, if he may chuse [*sic*] the Actors."[30]

Incensed by LeClerc's article, Hickes brought out in 1711 *Two Treatises, one of the Christian Priesthood, the other of the Dignity of the Episcopal Order, formerly written, and now publish'd to obviate the Erroneous Opinions, Fallacious Reasonings, and Bold and False Assertions, in a late Book, Entitl'd, The Rights of the Christian Church,* an impassioned accusation that the author of *The Rights* had tried to overthrow the constant doctrines of all ages; and another, well described in its title: *Spinoza Reviv'd: Or, a Treatise proving the Book Entitul'd, The Rights of the Christian Church &c (In the most Notorious Parts of it) to be the same with Spinoza's Rights of the Christian Clergy &c.* . . . The remainder of the overlong title asserted that both Spinoza's book and *The Rights* were "grounded upon downright Atheism."

In reply to the first, LeClerc adopted the tone of an elder by observing that Hickes had railed where he should have discoursed and that his deportment had been indecorous. LeClerc recognized that the privilege to rail was ordinarily accorded the loser and that, "It were to be wish'd, that upon this Occasion, [Hickes] had made use of softer Language, and mixt nothing of Personal in the Dispute." He said that had Hickes delivered his arguments quietly and in a manner befitting a churchman, they would not have lost their force, but by resorting to calling the author a papist and a "Sower of Sedition," he had given his adversary the right to reply in kind.

As for *Spinoza Reviv'd*, LeClerc had special contempt for it. He pointed out that Hickes had written only the preface and that the true author was an Irishman named Carol, who had been persuaded by Hickes to abandon the priesthood to embrace Protestantism. LeClerc said that this action in itself was sufficient reason to disqualify the treatise from serious consideration and went on to say that to call him a Spinozist on the basis of Carol's insipidity was nonsense. He forgave Hickes his odious language in the preface but did not forgive Carol his violent style and the irresponsible content of the treatise. He said that the best Carol had done was to cast aspersions on "those who are unknown to him."

William Wotton's sermon, *The Rights of the Clergy in a Christian Church*, against *The Rights* was preached at Newport Pagnel on September 2, 1706 and by the next year it had gone through four editions. Without discussing it, LeClerc praised Wotton for his relative moderation and tranquility. As for the four remaining pamphlets, he simply made brief mention of them—an attempt, perhaps, to display his impartiality. But his was an unconvincing neutrality.

In his review, he restated his adherence to the basic principles in *The Rights* and wrote, "I am, in truth, against *Tyranny* either in *Church* or *State*; and yet am for *Obedience* and *Peace*, provided *Truth* and *Law* be not sacrific'd to the Capricious Humour of *Men*" (p. 30). He further maintained his esteem for English government as established by law, for the Church of England, and for "all the Ingenious Men of that Nation."

To pursue the subject a little further, to reveal the depth and ramification of LeClerc's ability to stir British clergy and to show the extent of penetration of *Bibliothèque Choisie*, note must be made of three more pamphlets. The first, *A Second Defense of the Rights of the Christian Church... In a letter from a Gentleman in London to a Clergyman in the Country*, vigorously defended LeClerc's abstract. The writer liked his high regard of the British and approved the main points in the original work as LeClerc had presented them. This correspondent had identified himself as a "friend of W. Tindal" and strongly hinted that Tindal was the author of *The Rights*. The second, in the form of an epistle, shows that LeClerc's work aroused interest even among students. A young "Oxford-Scholar" reported that he had listened to a sermon by Dr. Moss in which *The Rights* had been attacked. Afterwards, the young man had felt that the author of the book had made a stronger case.[31]

The third, *A Narrative of the Prosecution of Mr. Sare...*, for *Selling the Rights of the Christian Church...*, proved that *The Rights* was so controversial that it was "arraign'd of Sedition, Rebellion, Blasphemy and what not" by conservative clergymen and that it had raised issues so inflammatory that zealous churchmen tried to identify the author and the printer in order to bring them to trial. In his narration, Samuel Hilliard, prebendary of Lincoln, said that on December 12 and 13, 1708, the prosecution had tried to get the names from Richard Sare, the bookseller, but that he had said that disclosure was a violation of the ethics of his profession. According to Hilliard, the Lord Bishop of London had urged vigorous prosecution on the grounds "that something ought to be done, since *Monsieur Le Clerk* [*sic*] had recommended it in his *Bibliothèque Choisie.*"[32]

These accounts of LeClerc's dealings with Cudworth's *The True Intellectual System* and with the anonymous *The Rights of The Christian Church Asserted* show the great influence of *Bibliothèque Choisie.* His success may be attributed in large measure to the correctness of his basic assumption that good books needed to be rescued from premature obscurity as in the case of *The True Intellectual System* or to be given wide readership as in the case of *The Rights.* Furthermore, he recognized the need for judicious extracts and, more importantly, for orderly, clear summaries. As a purveyor of other men's thoughts, as a commentator on them and as an advocate of the use of reason in pursuit of truth, he was the chief intermediary in the movement of theological debates from one part of the republic of letters to another.

VI *Science*

The new science, too, captured popular interest and LeClerc performed a great service by printing abridgments of the works of Isaac Newton and by including notices of the works of George Berkeley. LeClerc recognized the value of these two scientists but wisely refrained from dealing with their works with the confidence and familiarity with which he did in areas where he was more at home, as has already been noted.

His knowledge of Newton went back to 1688 when Locke had provided him with an abridgment he had written of *Philosophiae Naturalis Principia Mathematica,* which had appeared in London in 1687. LeClerc had printed the abridgment in *Bibliothèque Universelle et Historique,* Tome VIII, March, 1688, and even though he added no comment, had been instrumental in bringing to the Continent what was to become the greatest scientific work of the century.

How quickly Newton's work had reached readers may be seen in LeClerc's eulogy for his friend Burcher de Volder (1643-1709), professor of philosophy and mathematics at Leyden.[33] In this tribute, LeClerc wrote that De Volder had always been interested in new developments in the sciences and had read *Principia* with great zeal and excitement and that Huyghens, the mathematician, had confessed to De Volder that he had found Newton's ideas obscure. De Volder had replied that Newton was, indeed, hard and obscure but that, nevertheless, his principles were true.

In *Bibliothèque Choisie,* Tome IX, LeClerc printed a synopsis of *Opticks,* in which he recalled an earlier but tenuous relationship. Newton had asked Locke to arrange for his "Historical Account of two Notable Corruptions of the Scriptures, in a Letter to a Friend" to be translated into French and published in Holland. By this means he had hoped to avoid conflict with British churchmen and to have an appraisal of the work from biblical scholars on the Continent before he "put it forth in English." Locke had copied the manuscript in his own hand and had sent it without the author's name to LeClerc in Amsterdam, requesting translation and publication. LeClerc had agreed to undertake a Latin or a French translation himself because, as he had written Locke, "the work deserved publication." But Newton had changed his mind and had written to Locke from Cambridge, February 16, 1691/2, "Let me entreat you to stop their translation and impression so soon as you can, for I design to suppress them." In a letter dated April 11, 1692, LeClerc had replied to Locke's containing this decision by Newton. "It is a pity that these two dissertations should be suppressed."[34] Evidently Newton's fear of being known as the author had prompted the request but LeClerc had countered any possibility of violation of anonymity when he said that he could have given the work an "original air which would not have savoured of a translation." Locke had never told LeClerc the name of the author but it is possible that later he found out from the works of Whiston, who had mentioned the letters after Newton's death.

LeClerc's interest in publicizing Newton's work would carry over into *Bibliothèque Ancienne et Moderne.* It will be seen that in the first tome he inserted a brief synopsis of *Analysis per Quantitatum, Series, Fluxiones ac Differentias cum enumeratione*

Linearum tertii Ordinis and told readers that it could be bought at Mortier's bookshop where the second edition of *Principia Mathematica* (Cambridge, 1713) was also available. And in Tome XII, he would say he thought it valuable to announce a second edition, augmented, of *Opticks* in French translation, published in Amsterdam.

How important LeClerc may have been as an intermediary for Newton's work is open to question. While unknowledgeable in Newtonian scientific thinking, he had willingly accepted Locke's judgment and had printed the entire abridgment of *Principia*. Thus, he merits a secure place as a link in the dissemination of Newton's work. If LeClerc did not fully understand Newton, he certainly was sympathetic to his use of experiment in the new science and, especially, in his belief in Man's ability to discover truth by his own powers.[35]

Acting further as an intermediary in scientific thought, LeClerc brought to his readers the work of George Berkeley. There had been some correspondence between the two. Berkeley had written twice (March 28, 1711, and July 14, 1711) from Trinity College, Dublin. In the first letter he had presented a rough draft of *Discourse on Passive Obedience* and, in the second, fragments of what may have been meant for a sermon and a draft of *Principles of Human Knowledge*.[36] LeClerc's interest was in Berkeley's scientific work and in Tome XXI of *Bibliothèque Choisie*, listed among books to be dealt with in a later tome, *An Essay towards a new Theory of Vision* (1709) and in Tome XXII, under the rubric *Livres de Philosophie*, a detailed resumé, but, as in the case of Newton's work, without a single comment.

VII *LeClerc and Shaftesbury*

In 1699 the Third Earl of Shaftesbury made his first trip to Amsterdam where Locke introduced him to LeClerc. Later, Shaftesbury returned and remained there from August, 1703, to August, 1704, and until his death in 1713, they were close friends. LeClerc was attracted to Shaftesbury's writings and provided the first comprehensive review and commentary on *Characteristics* (1711) in three issues of *Bibliothèque Choisie* (Tomes XIX, XXI, XXIII). From the outset, LeClerc insisted that he did not know the identity of the author, but in view of the closeness of their relationship and of his knowledge of

Shaftesbury's earlier work, the statement does not ring true. His disclaimer is clouded and can be cleared only by the conjecture that he was respecting Shaftesbury's wish for anonymity.

LeClerc's articles, very important for spreading Shaftesburian thought to the Continent and for kindling more interest among his countrymen, were quickly translated into English and, one year after publication of *Characteristics,* LeClerc had accomplished the amazing feat of reviewing the book and of being essentially responsible for its appearance in pamphlet form. His reviews brought to the *literati* abstracts and judgments of a work he considered a major literary and intellectual triumph. Shaftesbury's prose style had caught LeClerc's attention and his delight was so great that he said that even good translation was impossible to do it justice. He said that whoever the author may be had written "avec beaucoup de délicatesse et de véracité." He was dazzled by the lively and noble expressions, citing as an example for purity and energy the dialogues of Theocles and Philocles.

In the review of "A Letter concerning Enthusiasm," he condoned its loose organization and casual approach by explaining that the author had used the genre of the epistle rather than that of the treatise. As for the French translation, he complained that its inadequacy had resulted in wrong sense in some places. In dealing with the contents, LeClerc explained that the author had been careful to distinguish between false or "outer" and true or "inner" forms of enthusiasm. "Inner" enthusiasm, LeClerc noted, was born from the love of truth and properly heightened the passions. Although he believed in the supremacy of human reason, he seemed to be willing to accept the Shaftesburian notion that true enthusiasm involved all the strange movements of the imagination whether founded on reason or not.

The review of *The Moralist* was hasty and brief. He said that the work was distinguished by such excellence in writing that "the *French* Tongue is but languid, in comparison" (p. 56) to the English and advised readers to consult the original instead of depending on the translation. The important truths in the discourses of the skeptic impressed him as did the attack on Hobbes. His concluding comment was general praise for the author's ease and freedom which, LeClerc promised, "will please so much the more as one penetrates the bottom of the Subjects, and enters into the Mind and Manner of the Author" (p. 5).

As part of the same article, he dealt with *Sensus Communis* and said it was written in beautiful English. Such emphasis on or consideration of prose style was a fresh element in LeClerc's reviewing. Having ignored literary style for so long, he now acknowledged that in itself it could be a force for intellectual expression. Yet in this case his ardor was misplaced in view of Shaftesbury's unsystematic handling of the material and of his esthetic rather than logical mode of presentation. On the other hand, LeClerc may have been lauding the style in an effort to persuade readers to turn to the original text. He thought that the attacks on Pyrrhonism initiated in *The Moralist* linked it with *Sensus Communis* and again tried hard to substantiate his ignorance of the identity of the author, saying that he had brought together these separate works not because he was certain of single authorship but because he had found in them correspondence of ideas and of manner of treatment.

In Tome XXI he continued his favorable review of *Characteristics*. In general, he liked *Soliloquy* but was most impressed by the singular "turn of the Whole" and the style "full of Spirit and Wit." In an illuminating statement in regard to Dutch lack of knowledge of English poetry, he wrote, "The *English* Poets indeed are not so well known to us, because few Men on this side [of] the Sea understand *English* well enough to read those poets" (p. 13). His own awakening to and his appreciation of British works which he had once considered of dubious value are noteworthy.

In reviewing "An Inquiry concerning Virtue ...," he said it was solid in matter, regular in method, and "as well handled as any Treatise of Morality I ever read in my Life" (p. 19). After giving a detailed outline, he urged that the author "ought to be applauded by all sensible Men" (p. 54), especially for his anti-Hobbesian defense against the thesis that the natural state of man was a state of war. He agreed that this notion was absurd and "foreign to all Society."

In the overview of *Characteristics*, LeClerc exhausted his vocabulary of praise for both style and content; he could go no further than to declare the author a "Master of his Language" and to state that the whole work was valuable mainly for its defense of liberty and virtue against the inroads of intellectual slavery and vice, "things which deserve the most to be abhor'd [*sic*] by Mankind" (p. 72).

Shaftesbury was, of course, well aware of the publicity attend-
ing *Characteristics* and especially of LeClerc's influence. *Miscellaneous Reflections* devoted a whole chapter to controversial
writings and treated the subject with mild irony. Shaftesbury
seemed to be pointing at the sort of writing that was dominating
the "learned scuffles" of LeClerc and his disputants. In Chapter
III, he looked directly at reviews by Basnage and by LeClerc
when he said that "The Protestant writers, such as live in a
free country, and can deliver their sentiments without con-
straint, have certainly done our author more honour than he
ever presumed to think he could deserve."[37] He showed that
he had read *Bibliothèque Choisie* carefully when he commented
on the nature of the epistolary style. He was paraphrasing
LeClerc when he complained about the abuse of this form
which had produced "the title of a private letter to a piece
addressed solely to the public" and then observed that "a chief
critic of the Protestant side," unmistakably LeClerc, "when
mentioning this letter concerning Enthusiasm, ... speaks of it
as a real letter ... not [as] a precise and formal treatise designed
for public view."[38]

In *Miscellany IV*, Shaftesbury referred to LeClerc as "a
learned critic and master in all philosophy, modern and ancient."
This lavish praise was partial repayment for support of his
argument concerning natural ideas which he had read in Le-
Clerc's recently published edition of the dialogues of Aeschines.
He was especially pleased with the remark, "They [some British
writers] seem indeed to be but weak philosophers, though able
sophists, and artful confounders of words and notions, who
would refute Nature and common sense."[39]

In *Miscellany V*, Shaftesbury used LeClerc for support in his
discussion of the Primitive Fathers. He quoted a long passage
from *Bibliothèque Choisie,* Tome XIV, and cited LeClerc as
"a foreign Protestant divine, and most learned defender of
religion, making the best excuse he can for the Greek Fathers,
and endeavouring to clear them from this general charge of
havoc and massacre committed upon science and erudition."[40]

Shaftesbury, by virtue of his own writings, and LeClerc, by
virtue of his recognition of their worth and of his success in
giving them great popularity, formed a good partnership in
the dissemination of British thought.

VIII *LeClerc and Addison*

LeClerc's relations with Joseph Addison were of long standing but on a more formal basis than was his friendship with Shaftesbury. Yet it will be recalled that he had felt free to solicit Addison's help when he had sought a place in England and that Addison had tried to be of assistance. When *Remarks on Several Parts of Italy* appeared, LeClerc wrote a detailed and enthusiastic article in which he admired the originality of thought and the excellence of literary style. Like so many other articles in *Bibliothèque Choisie*, this one quickly found its way to England via translation and appeared as a pamphlet entitled "Monsieur Le Clerc's Observations upon Mr. Addison's Travels Through Italy, etc. Also Some Account of the United Provinces of the Netherlands...."[41]

LeClerc described it as a work "so curiously turn'd, that 'tis difficult to determine whether the Author writes best in Prose or Verse" and said that Addison "passes with Reason for one of the Greatest Poets which *England* at this time boasts" (pp. 2-3). LeClerc told readers that this book provided a good way to recall agreeably places they may have visited, and also that it presented observations that may never have occurred to them. Placing this work in the same general class as travel books by Burnet, Ray, and Misson, he pointed out Addison's greater originality in ideas and his superiority in writing and noted especially the astute comparison of French and Italian "Humours" which, he believed, brought out the source of aversion between these nations. He was delighted with the observations on Italian opera, agreeing completely with Addison's approval of the music but his disapproval of all the rest, which were ridiculous "wretched Farces, full of lewd and witless Conceits" (p. 10).

He was pleased that Addison had taken only a slight view of St. Peter's and on the basis of this remark, took the opportunity to lash out at Rome. Contrasting its wealth with the poverty surrounding it, LeClerc suggested that the Church give relief to the "poor miserable People.... 'Tis ridiculous to imagine that God and the Saints ... take Pleasure in beholding such Magazines of Wealth ..., in the midst of a People so poor and distress'd.... The Catholic Church is the sole Cause of the Poverty of the Place" (pp. 13-16). He was reacting to Addison's view but his expression is bitter and hostile while Addison's is cool and urbane. The long article ended with mention of Addison's interest in medals and with the hope that he would oblige the public with a book on the subject.

This review was only the start of LeClerc's contribution in bringing Addison's writings to the Continent. As volumes of *The Spectator Papers* began to make their way into the literary world, LeClerc added his influence. His reviews and abstracts of them in *Bibliothèque Ancienne et Moderne* will be considered later.

IX   *Historiography*

Bibliothèque Choisie was a repository for more than reviews and commentaries on classical scholarship, theology, and literary essays; LeClerc expanded it to include historiography. The writing of history had long attracted his attention and his skeptical nature had made him doubt the accuracy and honesty of many historical accounts. By questioning the validity of the sources upon which contemporary historians relied, by urging that truth must always prevail even when the disagreeable and ugly might emerge, he tried to establish professional standards to rid historical writing of conjectures, old wives' tales, myths, and legends. He said that for this kind of writing, material must come only from authentic sources where objectivity and honesty prevailed. His pronouncement helped build a more solid foundation for a kind of writing sorely needed in his day. Heretofore, prejudice, guesswork, unexamined reports, and questionable honesty had prevailed. As he well knew from his editing of Moreri's *Dictionnaire Historique* and from his reading of contemporary historical works, perpetuation of errors had been rampant.

A case in point was the discussion of Sir William Temple's *Observations upon the United Provinces of the Netherlands,* a spirited account of his long experiences in Holland. LeClerc said that it contained errors which needed immediate correction and argued that the best time to remove them was while an author was still alive and before they became fixed in readers' minds. Repetition made remedy difficult. The errors in Temple's account appear slight but LeClerc felt they should not have been there at all. Temple had said that the Haarlemmermeer was fresh water; LeClerc told him that it was not. Then he disparaged Temple's reliance on cliché when he said, "never [had] any Country [Holland] Traded so much, and Consum'd so little." LeClerc said that this reference to Dutch frugality was a generalization without support and had no place in an objective account of a people. He corrected another misstatement —that the Arminians were a party in the State—and said that this serious error had to be removed at once.

A second example of LeClerc's campaign for a more responsible and professional attitude toward the writing of history was in the review of The Earl of Clarendon's *The History of the Rebellion and Civil Wars* in Tome XVIII. He found it a flawed work which failed to measure up to those standards essential to good historical writing. In his opinion, the author was too partisan for the Royal party, had overlooked deliberately or otherwise the problem of the Duke of York's religion, and had referred to himself too often. LeClerc said that the basic problem with this book was the confusion in the author's mind between the writing of history and the writing of memoirs. These were separate genres and to mix them led to obscurity and faulty reporting. Clarendon's book although called a history was, in fact, a memoir as evidenced by the overabundance of personal references in it. History needed much greater objectivity. To clarify his argument, LeClerc cited Edmund Ludlow's *Memoirs* to show how differently his account of Cromwellian times had been handled. After discussing these ideas on the writing of history, LeClerc wrote a long resumé with generous excerpts of Clarendon's work which started in Tome XVIII and ended in Tome XIX. He praised the author not for his ability as a historian but for his being the grandfather of two queens.

A minor event which resulted in an unexpected consequence gave LeClerc an opportunity to deal with another aspect of historiography. When Thomas Shadwell died in 1692, he was succeeded as poet laureate by Nahum Tate. Shadwell had held the posts of both poet laureate and historiographer royal as had Dryden throughout almost all of his tenure and it seemed likely that the tradition would continue. But Tate was given only one post and Thomas Rymer was appointed historiographer royal. This appointment was a sinecure of £200 per annum and it was highly improbable to think of it as anything more. Yet Rymer made much of it. He had seen the steady and jumbled

accumulation of treaties, letters, and other instruments of State
and had recognized the need to put into order this heap of
historical treasure. Encouraged by Lord Halifax and with the
help of a small band of workers, he began the enterprise which
eventually was to become a monument in historiography—
Foedera.

It was natural that this tremendous work would come to
LeClerc's attention. Lord Halifax, already acquainted with him,
sent the first five volumes for possible review. LeClerc recognized
Foedera as a much needed work for historians and as a project
worthy of the generosity of the Queen. He wrote an abstract
of the first volume and then turned over the reviewing of the
rest to Rapin.

Rapin continued writing the abstracts for *Bibliothèque Choisie*,
and the steady stream of reviews of the volumes as they came
out attracted attention on the Continent, especially in Holland.
The Pensionary Fagel, who appreciated Rapin's abstracts, ar-
ranged to have them collected and printed in one volume by
the States Printer at The Hague. For unexplained reasons only
about thirty copies were printed and the work became scarce.
However, in 1726 there appeared an edition by Stephen Whatley,
who had translated Rapin's abridgments as they had appeared
in *Bibliothèque Choisie*. This edition came out in monthly
installments and eventually as a four-volume work to which
was appended a biography of Rapin and details of LeClerc's
part in the enterprise.[42]

The writings of Temple, Clarendon, and Rymer were given
ample treatment in *Bibliothèque Choisie* but one of the most
important purposes for LeClerc's having used them was his
concern to help improve the writing of history. By so doing,
he exerted a strong enough force to have had his influence go
so far as to impress even Edward Gibbon. Thus, as intermediary
in the area of history and historiography, LeClerc provides one
more important example of his general participation to bring
to readers on both sides of the Channel the sort of information
that underlay the strong cultural ties among members of the
republic of letters.

After ten years of publication, LeClerc said that he was
ready and willing to quit this exhaustive work, but was persuaded
to continue and did so in *Bibliothèque Ancienne et Moderne*.

X Bibliothèque Ancienne et Moderne

Bibliothèque Ancienne et Moderne with LeClerc as editor was published by three different booksellers: in Amsterdam, by David Mortier from 1714 to 1719 and by R. & G. Wetstein from 1719 to 1726; and, in The Hague, by Pierre Husson from 1727 to 1728. The booksellers were much more in evidence in this journal than they had been in the other two. In almost every tome, LeClerc advertised where the books mentioned could be bought and just before /he relinquished editorship he announced that Husson was prepared to sell not only the twenty-six complete tomes of *Bibliothèque Universelle et Historique,* the twenty-eight of *Bibliothèque Choisie* and the twenty-nine of *Bibliothèque Ancienne et Moderne* but also the separate ones. This advertising is indicative of the continuing interest in all of his journals as well as witness to their popularity even when topical interest had all but disappeared.

This periodical, aside from stronger emphasis on the commercial aspect, revealed a shifting movement in readers' interests. Having recognized mounting awareness of English literary works among Dutch readers, LeClerc included many articles dealing with British authors. Serious studies in theology, philosophy, science, and in other areas held their places but reviews of literary works were more in evidence than they had been in his previous journals. The range and scope of *Bibliothèque Ancienne et Moderne* became wider and brought to Continental readers accounts of the writings of Addison, Steele, and Swift. In the light of their enduring places in the history of English literature and of their subsequent reputations, LeClerc was correct in his assessment of Addison and Steele. He saw Addison as the stronger intellect and the more astute critic in literary matters and considered Steele more inclined to the didactic and moralistic in criticizing contemporary society. As for Swift, LeClerc showed good critical judgment when he pointed out his skill in producing a unique brand of satire.

In Tome I LeClerc reviewed the first volume of *The Spectator Papers* and cited the French translation. The review followed the general form of the previous one on Addison in *Bibliothèque Choisie.* It praised his style and said that the quiet satire and irony produced a sardonic tone exceedingly difficult to capture in translation and that "Matières de railleries" were the trickiest to handle. In a digression he dealt briefly with translation of poetry, using *Paradise Lost* as an example of a work whose beauty would be totally destroyed by it.

As quickly as volumes of *The Spectator Papers* were translated into French, LeClerc reviewed them. In Tome IV he announced publication of the second volume and reported on the clarity with which Addison had described the customs of the century. In Tome V he noted that the two volumes were available at the shop of the Amsterdam bookseller David Mortier. When the third volume was printed, he reviewed it in Tome VIII. First he mentioned the earlier ones and then reported that *The Spectator Papers* were well known and widely sold. This review is significant because having already realized the stature of the man, LeClerc was confident enough to state that the best essays and discourses in the *Papers* were written by "l'Illustre Mr. Addison, présentement Secrétaire d'Etat à Londres, hors de la Grande Brétagne." He called special attention to the discourses (Numbers 411-421) on the pleasures of the imagination, found these worthwhile, and urged readers to become acquainted with them. In expanding the commentary, he dwelt on the value of the study of *belles lettres* as Addison had used them. He believed that this kind of study should not be isolated but should be an adjunct to living in the world. A man who is so immersed in *belles lettres* that he does not know what is going on is, as LeClerc bluntly put it, "bon à rien." The reason for this observation grew out of his admiration for Addison's having brought *belles lettres* into closer contact with other cultural disciplines for the improvement of critical and esthetic judgments.

In a brief note in Tome XVI, he announced that the French translation of the fifth volume of *The Spectator Papers* was for sale in Amsterdam at the bookshop of R. & G. Wetstein, repeated the notice in the next tome, and called these volumes "si belles et si fines."

His interest in Addison was supplemented in Basnage's *Nouvelles de la République,* for which LeClerc contributed in the issue for January and February, 1718, a review of the translation of the third volume. Here he remarked most favorably on Addison's appreciative essays on *Paradise Lost* and labeled the commentary "une critique fine et judicieuse du célèbre Poëme de *Milton,* intitulé *le Paradis perdu.*" He informed readers of Basnage's journal that Addison was the author of the critique on Milton and that he wrote over the letters C, L, I, O.

LeClerc's participation in *Nouvelles de la République* continued over a two-year period, 1716-1718, but the reason is obscure. A good guess is that he was willing to do the extra work in order to cooperate with David Mortier, the bookseller of both periodicals. On the other hand, as valid a guess is that he wished to publicize Addison's writings wherever possible.

LeClerc's efforts to make Addison's work better and more rapidly known at home and abroad bore fruit. In his book on Richard Steele, Calhoun Winton, quoting from Smithers's biography of Addison, wrote that LeClerc had called *The Campaign* "an incomparable piece in heroic verse. . . . We may justly affirm that . . . Mr. Addison, thus raised and supported by the nobleness of his subject, is as much superior to himself, as he is in his other pieces to the greatest part of the other poets of what nation soever. . . . The finest writers in England have executed, in the *Spectator*, all the force of their reflections, all the delicacy of style and all the fire of imagination that can be conceived."[43]

Inevitably, LeClerc served as intermediary for Richard Steele in *Bibliothèque Ancienne et Moderne*. In Tome I he announced "La Crise de Whigs par M. Richard Steele" and "L'Esprit de Whigs" and while he was neither so voluminous in commentary nor so lavish in praise of Steele as of Addison, he continued to keep Steele in the public eye. In Tomes II and IV, there appeared lists of books available at Mortier's including "Oeuvres diverses de M. Richard Steele, sur les Affaires de la Grande Bretagne, traduites de l'Anglois, Amsterdam, 1715." Tome VI introduced *"Bibliothèque des Dames . . .* publiés par Mr. le Chevalier R. Steele" by means of a short but favorable review which stressed the moral side of Steele's writings. LeClerc liked the good advice which could be beneficial to all who cared to read the essays. When the second volume came out in Janiçon's translation, LeClerc reviewed it in Tome XI and observed that much of its advice on proper education came directly from Locke's *Thoughts Concerning Education.*

A surprising but noteworthy entry in *Bibliothèque Ancienne et Moderne* was LeClerc's comment on Pope. In his article in Tome VII on "Essai sur la *Critique* imité de l'Anglois de Mr. Pope," he stated that he was handicapped in attempting a comparison of the French imitation with the original because he had not read the *Essay on Criticism*. That such a widely read man as LeClerc could make this confession may indicate that Dutch interest in British literature was still confined chiefly to prose. Nevertheless, he argued weakly that since the imitation concerned itself with important matters and had been well written, the original must, therefore, be good.[44]

Although interest in British prose was general abroad, the work of Swift had not been fully appreciated. *A Tale of a Tub* had long been neglected and when Justus van Effen had translated it into French, LeClerc reviewed it even though he was well aware of Swift's contempt for him. Very likely he had not forgotten the caustic remark in the Bickerstaff essay but did not mention it; he limited himself to calling Swift's work "une pure plaisanterie, qui avoit déjà paru en François." Van Effen's translation was, of course, a landmark. The preface was a masterful essay in which he saw *A Tale of a Tub* in a much truer light than had British churchmen. In general, LeClerc agreed and, through his review and commentary, played a strong supporting role in the growth of Swift's popularity on the Continent. The satire on Dutch scholarship and on short cuts to learning as offered in the *Bibliothèques* came perilously close to making LeClerc the exemplar, but in his own way he was in accord with the honesty he saw in the work and refrained from singling out these points as personal issues.

Although LeClerc understood and appreciated Swift's brand of satire and recognized the excellence of his style, he focused attention on the allegory and ignored the digressions. To begin with, he found the strange title baffling but knew that it was an ingenious one to indicate that the book was an attack on Hobbes's *Leviathan* and dismissed the notion that such a bizarre title could apply only to an old wives' tale. As for the book, he admitted that he was perplexed by the peculiar sort of jesting which permeated it and that he was often puzzled when he tried to distinguish the serious from the comic. Notwithstanding, he knew the sort of people under attack and informed readers that they, too, could identify the targets by reading "la Dédicace prétendue du Libraire à Mylord Sommers, celle de l'Auteur au Prince Posterité, la Préface et l'Introduction." Even though the whole atmosphere of the work was murky, existing under a deep, dark cloud, he attempted to pierce it and to throw some light on Swift's peculiar construction. He noted that its super-

ficially chaotic form was exactly the correct one since the
mingling of the ridiculous with the serious was Swift's way of
reflecting the state of mind of many Englishmen unwilling to
distinguish good from evil or incapable of doing so.

As for the allegory of the three brothers, LeClerc supported
Swift against those readers who saw it as destructive rather
than informative and noted that Swift often spoke the truth
in a style "aussi caustique, que burlesque." To these critics, he
replied in his own caustic way that when they had purged themselves of these flaws which Swift had satirized, then and only
then could they demand reparations.

The second volume of Van Effen's edition contained among
other works by Swift translations of *Operations of the Mechanical
Spirit* and *The Battle of the Books*. LeClerc considered these
as separate essays, divorced from *A Tale of a Tub*. He agreed
with Swift's general position in *Operations* but had some grave
reservations about the attack on Prophecy. He said that if Swift
had limited his attack to the Fanatics, he would have been
absolutely right, but "s'il va plus loin & débite des principes, qui
détruisent la veritable Prophétie, il est visible qu'il a tort." As
for style, he found the irony excessive and the allusions not
always "justes & regulières." In general, he praised the essay but
forewarned readers not to think that the ideas in it were necessarily in harmony with Swift's own convictions. He concluded
that on this basis it might be advisable to reserve judgment and
to think well of Swift since the ideas he projected were not so
bad as they seemed to appear.

The Battle of the Books interested LeClerc even though he
had said long before that he refused to get entangled in the
controversy of the Ancients versus the Moderns. He said that
there was nothing complicated here; it was a fable in which the
Ancients had overthrown the Moderns, with Bentley and Wotton
representing the losers. Where LeClerc's sympathies rested is
evident in his not having even mentioned the names of the
victorious Ancients. Yet, with praiseworthy objectivity, he reported it a good work. In summation, he wrote, "La hardiesse
de la fiction ne pouvoit guère être portée plus loin; & il n'y a point
de fables ancienne, qui égale celle-ci."

These brief observations on *A Tale of a Tub* were part of
the tortuous history of learning to understand Swift; their brevity

did not strip them of their value in teaching Continental readers
how to approach his work.

LeClerc approved of the rest of the essays in Van Effen's
edition, electing to stress the greatness of the satire he saw
in *Abolishing of Christianity*. He liked Swift's use of indirection
in it and warned those readers who might venture to read the
original that the prose would sound strange to foreigners.

The same tome which carried the review of *A Tale of a Tub*
had an article on Daniel De Foe's *Robinson Crusoe*. LeClerc
thought that De Foe, "assez connu en Angleterre," had produced
a moral novel exciting enough to destroy silly romances. Said he,
such a book was superior to "les Romans des Amours Chimériques
de Héros veritables" because it healed unruly passions that only
troubled mankind.

Reviews of these writings of British authors in *Bibliothèque
Ancienne et Moderne* performed a relatively small but useful
service in transmitting news of Addison, Steele, Pope, Swift,
and De Foe but even though these contributions were modest,
they were part of the mosaic of Anglo-Dutch cultural relations.
In the light of the popularity of this periodical, these articles
reached enough readers in Holland and elsewhere to give
prominence to British writers not yet familiar to the general
Continental public.

XI *Theological Writings*

When *Bibliothèque Ancienne et Moderne* started, LeClerc
was at the height of his reputation as a controversial figure
in criticism of the Old and the New Testaments. He had revised
the work of Hammond, had translated the New Testament, and
had explicated much of the Pentateuch. As a biblical scholar,
he damned legend, myth, and conjecture which led to groundless
beliefs and championed reasonable, scientific, and professional
standards which removed unchallenged obscurities.

His interest in exegesis is illustrated by his long review and
critical examination in Tomes XVI and XVII (1721) of Humphrey
Prideaux's *Connection of the Old and New Testament,* which
appeared in an English translation in 1722 and was dedicated
to the Earl of Nottingham. The writer of the dedication, who
identified himself as Philalethes, had referred to LeClerc as
"a Learned Foreigner" and had called attention to the publication

of the original article in Amsterdam and of a Dutch translation in Leyden.

LeClerc's review, an attempt to teach readers the proper
method for biblical criticism, developed into a miniature treatise
on the subject. He pointed out the need for absolute accuracy
and for adherence to sure authority. "When we lay down a
System which is not founded upon any certain Authority, or
conclusive Reasons, we ought to speak with some Doubt and
Shew [*sic*] of Uncertainty. Otherwise we run the hazard of
deceiving ourselves, and the more Consequences we pretend
to draw, the more we run the Risque of putting off Romance
for real History" (p. 39). In all his remarks on the writing of
history, he never tired of warning against overuse of conjectures
and of transmogrifying them into facts. So, here again, he
cautioned historians to guard against descending "into a Romance,
by joining too many ... Guesses together, and drawing Consequences from them" (pp. 44-45).

He praised Prideaux's use of both sacred and profane history
to explicate obscure passages and thought the work "useful
to all Degrees and Conditions of Men, who would know the
History of the Jews *and* Neighbouring Nations, *from the Declen-
sion of the Kingdoms of* Israel *and* Judah *to the Time of* Christ"
(p. 4). Prideaux's reliance on the pioneering work by the
celebrated Archbishop of Armagh, James Ussher, and on the
writings on chronology by Sir John Marsham won LeClerc's
endorsement. He found that Prideaux had presented his points
in "a Method so elegant and unperplexed, that it renders the
Perusal ... agreeable to every Reader" (pp. 5-6). He then dealt
with specific places in the text and in every case applied the
principles of the uses of reason and authentic evidence as the
only ways to rout errors. However, he objected to Prideaux's
statement that it was reasonable that Noah had fancied himself
a divine mediator and admonished the author and all biblical
historians that it was not sufficient to show that it was "a *Reasonable Opinion*" but that it was mandatory to prove conclusively
"that the People of that Age *actually held* such a *Doctrine*"
(p. 14). And later, he asserted that explicators of the Scriptures
must avoid looking for what they wished to find there "but to
believe what [they] *find*" (p. 24).

LeClerc's rigoristic views on historical writings in general
and on exegesis in particular, especially in correcting errors

which had passed as historical facts, were well illustrated in Driebergh's Dutch translation. Although LeClerc had stated that he would not discuss books by Dutchmen, in this instance he relented since Driebergh's scholarship was admirable and his translation, excellent. LeClerc found it "equally faithful and elegant, as all must allow that understand the *Dutch* Tongue" (p. 50). He said that Prideaux's work had been circulated in manuscript and "Monsieur *Vitringa,* the Elder, who [was] a very excellent Judge ... and whose Impartiality [was] universally confessed" (p. 51) not only approved of the manuscript but also of Driebergh's Dutch version. Vitringa found the whole work so impressive that he was pleased to express his admiration in the preface to Driebergh's volume. The reviews of Prideaux's book and of Driebergh's translation and commentary provide rare instances of LeClerc's discussing contemporary Dutch work.

When Bishop Burnet died in 1715, LeClerc wrote an essay to extol his virtues. Very soon after its appearance, it was translated into English and published as a pamphlet entitled "The Life of Dr. Burnet ... with his Character, and an Account of his Writings...." The review, an account of Burnet's life and works together with LeClerc's observations, reiterated some of the fundamental beliefs which ran through all the *Bibliothèques.* He praised Burnet's frank and open manner of expression and found it a valuable asset for the writer of history. "... 'tis a very noble Quality, and absolutely necessary to a good Historian. Shou'd those who undertake to write History be naturally reserved or timorous, or shou'd they stand too much upon a cautious Prudence or be acted by a Party Spirit, we are to expect nothing from them but perpetual Dissimulation and continual Disguise of Matters of Fact, not to mention the Falsities which they will needlessly broach,... (p. 37).

In addition, LeClerc stated his close contacts with scholarship, with universities, and with affairs of Church and State in England. He deplored those members of the clergy who insisted upon submission to "the Authority of the Church, and to obey her Orders, preferably to all humane Laws" (p. 7). His longest commentary was reserved for British universities. After admitting that academic establishments were useful and necessary, he said that he had heard that British universities were "no better than Seminaries of idle People, who have no regular Method of studying, and who are industriously imbu'd with such Principles as are so far from being proper to render the civil Society happy, and to edifie [*sic*] a Christian Congregation, that they are fit for nothing but to make a Prince continually uneasie, if he will not enter into the cruel and outragious [*sic*] Measures of non-tolerating Theologues. If this Report be not true, I congratulate them upon it with all my Heart" (p. 30).

But he praised university scholars for their output of fine editions of the classics and noted that "it is certain that when the *English* do seriously apply themselves to any thing, they succeed perfectly well in what they undertake. I have never fail'd to do Honour to their Learning and Penetration, both in the *Bibliothèque choisie* and in this present *Bibliothèque*, and several *English* Gentlemen have testified their Obligations to me upon that Account" (p. 31).

However, he looked askance at English writers in general and said that on the Continent there was complaint that in most cases they "observe but little Method in their Writings, express themselves in an incorrect manner, and do not improve so much as they ought by the reading of foreign Authors, who to their Learning generally add a good Stile and a regularity of Thought" (pp. 31-32).

In its decade of publication, *Bibliothèque Ancienne et Moderne* dealt with many other works but these examples are representative of LeClerc's campaign to establish new standards for the writing of all kinds of history, most importantly, ecclesiastical history, where too much had been accepted as fact without proper examination. Through his examples in his independent historical writings and through his articles, he enunciated principles which eventually became standards for all responsible historians.

Bibliothèque Ancienne et Moderne brought to a close LeClerc's long career as a journalist. The three periodicals form a vast source of information on contemporary views, especially those held by the less orthodox. In them LeClerc emphasized British works because the general movement of cultural activity flowed most strongly from England to Holland.

However, the British had not yet developed cosmopolitan journals so influential as LeClerc's and, accordingly, had to be rescued from parochialism by journalists already firmly established; xenophobia had been their stumbling block. LeClerc's quick recognition of ideas which contained truths based on the use of reason and his willingness to support them against vigorous opposition accounted in good measure for the rapid popularity of Burnet, Shaftesbury, and Addison on the Continent. They constituted an important force in the ascendancy of modern ideas.

As for the Dutch, the case was different. They had not remained passive; they had not resisted learning English and, therefore, could read works in the original. Of more importance, their hospitable climate for tolerance and their loosening of the strong bonds of tradition had led to a cosmopolitan outlook receptive to foreign thought. They may have gone a bit too far because they had sacrificed their language and had lost some of their national identity but, in the long run, the loss was superficial.

LeClerc did not singlehandedly shape the course of events leading to the easier acceptance of ideas so bitterly opposed and so energetically defended in his day, but, as a journalist, paved part of the road on which reason, tolerance, and professional standards in scholarship moved to the great benefit of the republic of letters.

CHAPTER 4

Other Works

"I take upon me absolutely to condemn the fashion-
able and prevailing custom of inveighing against
critics as the common enemies, the pests and in-
cendiaries of the commonwealth of Wit and Letters.
I assert, on the contrary, that they are the props
and pillars of this building; and that without the
encouragement and propagation of such a race, we
should remain as Gothic architects as ever."

LECLERC'S three *Bibliothèques* are a monumental work and
his others are so voluminous that all together they form a
tribute to his stamina, industry, and interests. With more than
seventy other works to his credit he was not exaggerating when
he said that from schoolboy days he never went three days without a book or pen in his hand. He was well aware, too, that so
much publication could lead to charges of superficiality, but he
belonged to that astonishing group of polymaths whose range of
interest, depth of knowledge, and intensity of purpose impelled
them to write tirelessly. In defense of his great outpouring of
works he said, in Tome XXVII of *Bibliothèque Ancienne et
Moderne,* that he had been forced to do so much writing because
others had done so little. Characteristically, he chided those who
had great leisure and knowledge but wrote nothing for forcing
others like himself to serve the public as well as they could. He
spoke out against his critics and said that they had read fewer
books than he had written and that they were like elephants,
producing an offspring once in ten years.

As in the case of the *Bibliothèques,* many of LeClerc's other
works had appeared originally in French, had been published in
Holland, and then had been translated into English. By this
familiar route they played dual roles in spreading his thought.

I Parrhasiana

The best way to appreciate LeClerc as an intermediary is to
examine *Parrhasiana,* a work too long neglected.[1] It is a series of

105

essays on a variety of subjects closely allied to and anticipating those found in his journals. Here LeClerc, disguised as one Theodore Parhasse, used the forms of the essay and miscellany in much the same fashion as did Addison and Shaftesbury. Quickly, *Parrhasiana* found its way to England in translation and its success encouraged LeClerc to write a second part but, like so many sequels, it did not live up to the first and has remained untranslated and ignored.

Part One is composed of ten separate essays varying in length from two pages to more than fifty on such topics as criticism, history, morality, and politics. The idea of a miscellany of this scope developed, according to LeClerc, from a request of "a certain Person, who was chiefly concern'd in the Administration of the Republic of *Amsterdam*,"[2] to translate into French his Latin treatise against poetry. When this writer had asked LeClerc to comment on this treatise, he had resolved to write his own miscellaneous animadversions following the illustrious examples of Pascal, La Bruyère, Scaliger, Valesius, and others.

The first essay, "Of Poets and Poetry," was a plea for readers to see the Ancients and the Moderns in a light unclouded by adulation or blurred by the remarks of the grammarians. Not denying the greatness of Homer and of Virgil, LeClerc applied his own brand of reason and of logic in an effort to reveal them stripped of conjecture and wishful interpretation. Here he was expressing ideas fairly common in England and in Holland. His views were not far from those of Pierre Bayle on demythology nor contrary to those of Shaftesbury, who viewed the Ancients as dealers in questionable morality. On the topic of *utile et dulce*, LeClerc favored *utile* and dismissed *dulce* as unworthy of serious discussion even though he was later to modify his stand.

With stern warning, he opened his discussion by defining a poet as a writer of fiction capable of beguiling the reader by "the glittering Pomp of his Expression" and by "the Harmony of his Cadence" (p. 2). He admonished that to read poetry was "to read the Work of a Liar" (p. 2). Although this bold statement indicated a long, unrelieved attack on poetry, LeClerc turned the essay toward an evenhanded discussion of the differences between ancient and modern poets. He found the Ancients useful in providing excellent lessons in morality and in politics "deliver'd in handsom[e] Terms and in Verse ... [which made] a ... lasting Impression upon [the] Memory" (pp. 2-3).

Their nobility of style was worthy of emulation to speak in "a lively and animated manner" (p. 3). However, he said that to read them only for amusement ought not to be looked upon as a serious occupation. As for the Moderns who wrote in Latin and Greek, they resembled the Ancients "just as Apes may be said to resemble Men" (p. 3). He contended that by borrowing excessively from the Ancients, by plundering their thoughts and by mindless imitation, the Moderns produced such vapid Latin and Greek poetry that nobody took them seriously. Even schoolboys were directed to the Ancients and were protected from the Moderns.

LeClerc urged the Moderns to disengage themselves from this servility by abandoning Latin and Greek in favour of their mother tongue and by writing on current subjects in modern idiom. By following this advice he said that the poet could become "an Original." Optimistically, he imagined a modern Homer who could dethrone the pedants and who could rid poetry of much needless classical ornamentation. He prophesied that in the republic of letters this putative poet, greater than Homer, would surpass the Ancients by modeling his "Poetry a-new by the Ideas of good Sense, which are infinitely better understood at present than they were formerly" (p. 5). Good sense would rid poetry of "that absurd Trash of the Pagan Divinities" (p. 5) and would replace it with truths. For signs of encouragement he cited Corneille, Boileau, Racine, La Fontaine, and Fontenelle as poets whose works were as outstanding in the contemporary world as had been the works of the Ancients in their own time.

Having separated the Ancients from the Moderns, LeClerc proceeded to merge both and considered the disadvantages arising from reading any poetry. He declared that poets, full of false thoughts, corrupted or weakened sound judgment and good taste and, without order in their thinking, depended only on imagination. Consequently, the reader succumbed to the lure of rhetoric and believed an argument cogent when, in reality, it was only a figure of speech.

Style was an important element in LeClerc's criticism and, in this essay he carefully distinguished the written from the oral. The former, he said, must avoid expressing pedestrian ideas in elevated tones; the latter must shun rant and bombast, especially in pulpits, if it is to be persuasive. He pointed to many pamphlets which were transcripts of sermons as examples in which the oral style differed from the written. He warned that these publications were seldom successful. "If [a clergyman] is ever so ill advised as to publish a Work of this nature, 'tis ten times worse for him; for a Reader is infinitely more rigorous than an Auditor" (p. 8).

LeClerc developed his essay by arguing that correct judgment of any discourse in prose or poetry could be made by applying three standards: Matter, Order, Style. The first was uppermost in his mind as he accused both Homer and Virgil of presenting barbarous and indecorous actions and fabulous events. He remonstrated against blind adulation and said that these "Fictions are not wonderful, but altogether ridiculous" (p. 11). He went on to say that if readers and critics tolerated excesses in the Ancients, they had to apply the same standard to modern romances.

The order of material by the device of *in media res* had his approval insofar as Homer and Virgil were concerned. Yet he found it necessary to point out flaws. Following Adrian de Valois, LeClerc went to great lengths to show Virgil's error in first making Ascanius old enough to have been a hunter of big animals and then young enough to have been dandled on Dido's knee. But, he said, such contradictions were minor and easily overlooked.

As for the third standard, style, LeClerc said that it pleased the reader of poetry but only when expression was "pure, proper, and simple" (p. 14) and when figures were ". . . drawn from the most elevated and beautiful things, so that they fill the Mind with nothing but noble and sublime Ideas" (p. 14). But, he added, the poet must be cautious not to overuse figurative language because the intrusion of improbability and impossibility was *"To throw the House out of the Windows"* (p. 17). As an example, he cited Virgil's picture of the Cave of Winds.

There was a place in poetry for the wonderful and the probable and LeClerc used Aristotle for his authority. However, this topic was left undeveloped as he continued to belabor poets in general. While they had license to manipulate language to achieve cadence and rhyme, they were often handicapped because they could not present exactly what they wanted to convey without spoiling rhyme or diction. At times they were forced to fill out lines not for the sake of something which needed saying, but simply to conform to the rules of their art. In these cases, there was superfluity of words with no addition to sense.

In LeClerc's opinion, one of the most glaring faults among poets was their dishonesty in flattering great leaders. This failing was evident even in Virgil, Horace, Ovid, and Martial. LeClerc said it was hypocritical to place Augustus among the gods while he was still alive. He refuted Horace's defense of poets as writers of fulsome panegyrics by calling Pindar a dissembler who wrote poems of praise only because he "was as greedy a Wretch as a Man well cou'd be" (p. 27). He took further issue with Horace's weak defense and said that poets ought not to be exempt from the vices of the rest of mankind.

Poets as moralists were suspect even though Horace had said that they were capable of instilling good qualities in the minds of children. But LeClerc felt that children were influenced by their teachers who were very often mere grammarians blindly adoring the Ancients. "They made their Children learn *Homer*, he that speaks of the Gods not only as bare Men, but even as vitious [*sic*] Men" (p. 30). Although some Ancients elevated young minds in matters of morality, LeClerc cited Ovid, Catullus, and Horace, whose uncensored works contained "filthy Stuff."

His adverse remarks on the use of classical poetry as models of good morals were summed up in this observation: "If we therefore find in the Poets some Passages that are Good, . . . we likewise find in them abundance that are vicious . . . without giving us any certain steddy [*sic*] Rules to discern Bad from Good" (p. 35).

In an ironic aside he wondered why poetry was more fit for prayer than was prose, as some Ancients had stated. He asked, ". . . did they believe that the Divinity wou'd be sooner affected by a pompous Discourse in Metre than by a simple Prayer in Prose?" (p. 36). He questioned the actions of poets who assigned to themselves quasi-religious roles and extraordinary powers and concluded that they only tried to inflate the value of their art by spreading the notion that the Deity preferred verse to prose.

To develop the point that if poets may be queried in matters of private greed and of dubious morality they must also be examined regarding their literary intentions, LeClerc focused on the epic poets. He said that Virgil had not written solely to instruct and that diversion had been his main design. He argued that Le Bossu's definition of a heroic poem as *"a Discourse invented with Art to form the Manners by Instructions disguised under Allegories...*" (p. 42) was not true since no one could prove that the contrary was not the case. He said that good moral instruction could be found almost everywhere among writers who had not the slightest intention of going beyond the telling of a romantic tale. If a writer wanted his work to be considered didactic, he should so inform his readers; otherwise, they were to assume that pleasure was his only purpose.

This sort of approach to the classical epics inevitably forced LeClerc to conclude, "... 'tis certain that there is nothing in *Homer* or in *Virgil* that can convince us that they design'd to instruct us in certain moral Doctrines" (p. 43). He recognized that good instruction in the epics was incidental "embroidery of the Fable, and not the principal Design of the Poet" (pp. 45-46) and that if instruction had been the primary aim of Homer, it was also the case for Scudéry and for Calprenède. As if to defend his shaky position, he undertook to consider the allegorical aspects, easily the source of conflicting interpretations. He sided with those who contended that an allegory able to produce different meanings was "no longer an Allegory, but a Riddle" (p. 48).

After consideration of poets in general and epic poets in particular, LeClerc commented on Aristotle and the playwrights. He attacked the instructional and moral value of tragedy and doubted the validity of Aristotle's catharsis. As far as he was concerned, philosophers were to be commended for having tried to find lessons of morality in the tragedies, but the fact was that the tragedians "busied their Brains to procure the Applause of the People and their Diversion..." (p. 51). LeClerc mentioned comic poets, too, and treated them with little respect. "The Comic Poets seem to have nothing else in view but to divert the Public, and to get Reputation and Mony [*sic*] by diverting them" (p. 52).

Having dealt with the aims of poets and playwrights, he concluded his essay in a surprisingly temperate manner. Quoting from Horace's *The Art of Poetry*, he disapproved of the description of the writer as one who mixed the useful and the entertaining while providing good advice, and ended by observing darkly that he was "mightily afraid that such a Poet has for a long while been nothing else but a pure Idea without reality" (p. 54).

LeClerc's criticism of the Ancients indicated that the so-called neo-classical world had some divisive elements. To study Homer by day and by night had its adherents, but there were those who chose to look at Homer as a human and not as a mirror of Nature. No doubt, LeClerc could be successfully attacked, but his criticism was predicated on acceptance of principles of logic and of dependence on strictly literal meaning. Given these basic conditions, his argument was valid—as valid as that of his British contemporary, Thomas Rymer, in his criticism of *Othello*.

Obviously, LeClerc's position was neither literary nor esthetic; it was one based on the insistence on absolute clarity of meaning. His view necessarily devalued the classics and deflated the poets. But he was not alone; he reported that many Amsterdammers had approved of his remarks in this essay and nowhere in the republic of letters were there more knowledgeable people than in Holland. How acceptable his anti-classical remarks were in England cannot be readily measured, but Shaftesbury, if he is representative of contemporary thought, said much the same thing in a general way—especially about the poet as a writer of fiction. The mere fact that *Parrhasiana* was quickly translated into English and enjoyed wide readership indicated interest in if not complete acceptance of LeClerc's stance.

In the first essay LeClerc had turned the Ancients on themselves by using examples from their works to expose their weaknesses but in the second, "Of True and False Eloquence," he made full use of them to support his commentaries. This essay is an ideal example of an orderly, clearly expressed, and forcibly argued work. Here LeClerc was not so much a commentator as a teacher and a gadfly. In his straightforward, unrelenting way, he examined eloquence as an art in itself but one very close to that of writing since both forms had as their aim the enunciation of truth. False eloquence put lies where truths should have been and truth became lost in darkness. He defined true eloquence as the art of speaking "to convince reasonable Men, to render them attentive, and to affect them... while we speak the truth" (p. 54).

He divided the subject into four sections: Invention, Disposition, Expression, and Pronunciation. Each was a brief lecture in which he tried to instruct readers on how to improve their critical judgment of what they read, but more, of what they heard.

Invention was judicious and not capricious selection of thoughts; poor use of invention resulted in emphasis on the unimportant

and the unessential while ignoring or understating the salient.
He found this condition rampant among preachers ignorant of
the rules of the art of eloquence who had learned their profession
by "Rote and Custom" and pointed out that many of them held
the stupid notion that talking a great deal was enough to provide
the stamp of good eloquence. As he so bluntly put it, "To be
able to talk an Hour or too [sic] about a Trifle ... seems to be
the finest thing in the World, provided a Man does not hesitate
but runs glibly on, and moves his Auditors" (p. 56). Writers,
too, were included as LeClerc wryly pointed to those who
thought large books were synonymous with good ones. Talking
and proving were different matters and he quoted Sallust's
epigram to clinch the matter. "Words enough, but little good
Sense" (p. 57).

On the other hand, he stated that discourses using true
eloquence formed clear presentations of ideas or arguments to
be proved and took for supporting material only "the most
simple, the most direct, and the most sensible" (p. 57). They
were necessarily of varying lengths—a slight subject needed slight
treatment; an important one demanded long examination. But
he observed that too many preachers failed to follow this simple
rule and talked endlessly on barren material. Their second fault
consisted in confusing the Possible with the Probable and the
Probable with the True and, as a result, their arguments became
entangled in ambiguity. Only logic and the "inviolable Light of
good Sense" (p. 59) must prevail. Dogmatically, he stated that
"There is no Authority in the World that can make Arbitrary
Laws for good Reasoning" (p. 59) and its rules must be obeyed.
He observed that many churchmen fell into the trap of using as
models for eloquence the works of the Primitive Fathers. "This
[was] one of the most crying Sins of Ecclesiastical Eloquence,
as 'tis managed in those Places where the Fathers are the Copies
they [the clergy] write after. A Man ought to leave his Reason
and Logic behind him in the Church-Porch to be edified with
such Preaching" (p. 60).

Their third fault was the abuse of reason. Often when reasons
seemed just, they were not really so because they failed to deal
directly with the subject. There was a difference, he insisted,
between "proposing to prove" and proving. In his opinion, the
expert practitioner of true eloquence knew that the first step was
to present his subject as clearly as possible and then to move

ahead along the straightest and best road. The less capable
were obscure because they tried to appear eloquent in an effort
to impress a listless audience. Of the inept, he said one should
not be surprised "if the uncertain Multitude blunder and grope
their way at mid-day, without knowing what Road they should
take, or implicitely [*sic*] follow the first Man they meet" (p. 67).

LeClerc discussed disposition of material and found that this
subject had been so neglected that many books, sermons, and
philosophical writings were, for the most part, "mere Confusion
and Chaos." He cited Plutarch and Seneca as examples. The
Primitive Fathers, too, were muddy because they had imitated
classical writers. But LeClerc excused his contemporaries because
it seemed to him "an undeniable Truth, that . . . we very much
surpass the Ancients, whatever the Admirers of Antiquity may
pretend" (p. 69). He credited Descartes with the rediscovery
and with the application of the rules of the art of eloquence and,
at the same time, paused to tell readers that he, too, had treated
this subject in his *Logic*, "printed twice at *Amsterdam* within a
Few Years." Then, playing the role of instructor, he advised
writers that the rules were most useful because they automatically produced definite plans of work which could be handled
successfully "with all the ease imaginable" (p. 71).

Under the third general heading, Expression, he said that
instruction required a simple style; excitement of pleasures
needed "an Elocution somewhat more raised" (p. 77); and moving of passions demanded a sublime style. Thus, following
Horace, LeClerc repeated the classical dictum of style suiting
matter which he called "an inviolable Law." Analyzing the
equipment of a truly eloquent man, he noted the absolute necessity of perfect command of the mother tongue as well as of dead
and foreign languages. He insisted that solid eloquence called for
clear, simple prose because the principal end of proper writing
and speaking was to be understood. The ". . . first thing we should
endeavour to obtain, is a Habit of Speaking so well, that the
Hearers may not only divine our Thoughts, but likewise that it
may not be possible not to understand them, when we have no
design to speak obscurely" (p. 79). Some speakers, especially
declaimers, as had been common among the Primitive Fathers,
had perpetually indulged in harangues because they lived at a
time when a high premium was placed on ornament of expression.

Taking a page from Locke's book on educating the young, LeClerc wrote that all the foregoing advice was pointless until a proper environment had been established in which young people could hear correct speech and avoid bad habits derived from being among those who expressed themselves in a slovenly manner. To help create a healthy milieu, he suggested maintenance of schools at public expense where youth could learn modern languages. He was astonished that none existed anywhere because every nation wanted its own language spoken well; he also pointed, it seemed, to England when he remarked that some nations had gone to great lengths to polish their own language.

On the subject of writing well, he repeated the frequently observed remark that unknowledgeable people thought that clear, orderly writing was easy while pomposity and bombast were reserved for genius. For support he turned to the Ancients and claimed that it was easier to imitate the "Hydropic Sublimity of *Seneca* or *Lucan,* than the unaffected simplicity of *Terence*" (p. 80). Then, looking at the Moderns, he commented that Brébeuf had translated Lucan's *Pharsalia* in a style as bloated as the original and that he could never have composed anything in the clear, unaffected style that Molière had used in *Misanthrope.* He said that he was following similar observations made by Cicero in *The Art of Oratory* and by Horace in *The Art of Poetry.* He reiterated that proper style was composed of clear expression, of metaphors, and of other figures that illustrated meaning in a naturally inevitable way and that its principle value was to avoid obscurity. He never tired of pleading for clarity; to him it was the "Language of Truth."

True eloquence was dependent on the fourth principle, Pronunciation. LeClerc, following the precepts laid down by Michel Le Faucheur in *An Essay upon the Action of an Orator,* a work he had praised as a masterpiece of its kind, said that a speaker "ought to follow Nature ... [as] polished by a Gentleman-like Education, and by conversing with Persons of good Breeding" (p. 91) and that he should follow the tenor of his discourse. Under this heading, LeClerc also included Le Faucheur's comments on gestures. He probably had in mind preachers who combined improper pronunciation with excessive physical movements and noted that those who waved their arms were making gestures "only good to drive away the Flies" (p. 92).

The summation of this essay was that false eloquence concealed truth and betrayed auditors, who came away from sermons unenlightened and, what was worse, uninstructed. Much of the trouble was that speakers and writers hid behind false eloquence in order to avoid speaking the truth and that the reason for this state of affairs was timidity growing out of fear of making enemies. His final statement was a trenchant one. "But when should we speak Truth, tho' the most important in the World, if we were to stay till it wou'd make us Friends among the generality of Mankind? Perhaps never" (p. 97).

Much later, in defense of the writings of Archbishop Tillotson, he would still expound on the low state of true eloquence and on Tillotson's mastery of the art. "Every Body knows that Sermons are commonly fill'd with a flashy Rhetoric, which takes much better from the Pulpit than the Press" (p. 3). But LeClerc would say that Tillotson's sermons were superb even in print because they were exact and free from inaccurate reasoning. This defense was evidently written for the benefit of the Dutch and, therefore, LeClerc quoted at length and commented on the sermon "Eternity of Hell Torments," a work probably unknown at that time in Amsterdam and one which carefully adhered to the rules of true eloquence.

In the first two essays, LeClerc had emphasized that search for truth through use of reason was essential in all honest discourse. He firmly believed that since reason never changed, it was the only reliable touchstone for proper understanding. His interests in chronology and in historical interpretations led him to write many commentaries and explications in which he dealt with the problems of what went into acceptable historical writing. One aspect of this very large subject resulted in "Of History and the Difference between the Modern and Ancient Historians."

As in the essay on eloquence, his preoccupation with orderly treatment yielded only to his zeal for the search for truth. Always before him were the ugliness and the cowardice of those fearful of facing it and, what was more appalling, their deliberate attempts to falsify. He excused unintentional errors but fiercely opposed repetition of unsubstantiated arguments and insupportable information. He said that history was entertaining and instructive when honestly written but that it was "infamous and hurtful" when full of dissembling and lying. He accepted the poet as a liar with much more tranquility and sympathy than he

did the historian. Historians should treat equally the laudable and
the deplorable; history was not a record of what one wished
but of what actually had occurred. He said that the prerequisites
of the ideal historian were mastery of subject, expertness in
writing honestly, skill in narrating information and understanding in forming true judgments. He charged the ideal historian
with the responsibility to be skilled in many languages, to be
conversant with forms of government, with contemporary interests and with the "Genius of the People." He reminded him
to exercise diligence and strict attention in order to arrive at
solid judgments and said that lacking even one of these attributes
could lead to failure. He used as examples the histories of France,
England, and Holland which he found deficient in dealing with
religion and politics where differences of opinion had obscured
facts. Forestalling criticism that he was too demanding, he
stated that very few men had the necessary qualifications to be
historians; writing good history was one of the most difficult of
tasks. To those who argued that a writer might be unable to
evaluate material properly even when he sincerely searched for
truth, LeClerc replied that the historian admitted his uncertain-
ties and his doubts; he "is not oblig'd to recount everything, ...
He is only oblig'd not to relate any thing that is false for true, and
not warrant any thing that is incertain [*sic*]" (p. 103).

In discussing mastery of subject, LeClerc differentiated history
from memoirs and, on this point, was following Cicero's recognition of the danger of such confusion. As he was to complain in
his comments on Clarendon's history, he said here that memoirs
were unreliable as history because they were always personal
and tried hard to leave a favorable impression for posterity. They
must, therefore, be weighed very carefully before being used as
first-hand, authoritative source material. He also said that caution
must be applied to the use of reports made to princes and to
generals and cited a familiar example in the case of Caesar, whose
commentaries, which were often considered history were, in
reality, only careless and irresponsible memoirs.

Having narrowed the sources of material, LeClerc was forced
to ask, "What course then shall an Historian take to inform himself of the Truth?" (p. 100). He replied that the only sensible one
was familiarity with reports of the people, with accounts from
all sides—friendly and hostile—and with Public Acts. Then, after
comparison, the historian might arrive at incontestable facts.

But he stressed that where material was dubious, it should be handled in general terms in order to avoid deceiving readers with unwarranted history. The problem was made even more difficult when the historian undertook a work based on information given by witnesses long dead. Here he had to bring to bear all the discernment possible in reading accounts, being particularly suspicious of those which seemed either stuffed with lies or replete with passion.

LeClerc praised the Ancients who had been extremely scrupulous in trying to be honest. In the works of Dionysius of Halicarnassus, Livy, and Polybius all sides of accounts had been expertly weighed. In his opinion, modern historians were far below their level. One, he said, always described France as victorious; another narrated the same history and insisted that France had been "drain'd and dispeopled to all Eternity" (p. 107). In a short digression he said that he might be open to criticism for having mentioned a war so recently concluded but argued that "A Man must have a very mean Opinion of the People... to think they are uncapable [*sic*] of hearing the least truth.... For my part, I don't believe them to be so unreasonable" (p. 107).

Citation of sources and of their reliability were next discussed and LeClerc came to the conclusion that "The Republic of Leters [was] at last... a Country of Reason and Light, and not of Authority and implicit Faith, as it has been but too long" (p. 108). Although citations had some worth, he recognized the folly and the absurdity of their overuse, saying that not many readers had access to all the books cited or, even if they did, very often had not read them. Yet he knew that lack of citations might create distrust causing readers to refuse to finish reading books which they thought might be undependable. He said that the bad historian frequently cluttered his book with a "pompous Catalogue of Authors... for Ostentation" (p. 110) and observed that nothing was easier than "to compose a great List of Historians whom we never beheld, and to place them boldly at the Head of a History" (p. 111). For an example, he cited Varillas, "whose Passion and Romancing Genius [were] conspicuous in every Line of his Works" (p. 111).

Next, in dealing with the historian's problems to instruct himself in truth and to present his findings without prejudice, LeClerc acknowledged the virtual impossibility of absolute objectivity by citing the disparity in contemporary accounts of the recent wars and warned that only disengagement from all passions could insure honest history. For support, he referred to Lucian's insistence on impartial treatment of friend and foe, and to Hugo Grotius, a rare and truly objective historian, who, in his history of the Low Countries, had treated Prince Maurice of Nassau as impartially as if the two men had never quarreled.

LeClerc believed that special attention had to be given to ecclesiastical history. In a satiric vein, he advised the historian to defend orthodoxy and never heresy for, if he were foolish enough to favor heretics ever so slightly, he must be prepared for attacks by zealots of orthodoxy. He said, mockingly, let the prudent historian follow the precept "That all that may be honourable in *Heretics* is false, and that all that is said to their Disreputation is true.... every thing that can do honour to the *Orthodox* is undoubted, and all that reflects upon them is a downright Lie" (p. 125). Since many had followed such a course either through cowardice or through prejudice, he drew the almost heretical conclusion that much ecclesiastical history needed reexamination before proper assessment could be made of where truth really rested.

Style was extremely important to LeClerc, as may be recalled from what he had said on the subject in the two previous essays. As in eloquence and in poetry, so in history style must be pure, clear, concise, simple, and natural. He said that the historian had no need for literary ornaments and for exotic allusions; his sole task was to tell what had happened and he agreed with Lucian that truth was the regulator of historical narration. He reminded the historian that figures should be used sparingly and that style should be elevated only with extreme caution. On the other hand, he pointed out that Quintilian had presented the opposing opinion—that style ought to be "more elevated than that of an Orator, and almost Poetical" (p. 131). When he turned to modern historians, he found a barbarous style in Aubigné and a less than acceptable one in Mézeray, whose otherwise excellent history of France could have been vastly improved by the use of purer and more polished language. He said that the elaborate and declamatory styles of John Baptist Nani and Emanuel Tesauro were to be avoided. He insisted that style and clarity go together and that obscurity was the chief enemy preventing widespread reading of history. "Good Thoughts need not be made obscure to appear good to those that under-

stand them; and the Reader, who is forced to stop every moment
to find out the meaning, is not at all obliged to the Historian who
gives him this trouble" (p. 134). His remarks on style ended
abruptly because he felt that this essay was not the proper place
for its full and exhaustive discussion. For more, he referred readers to Gerard John Vossius's *De Arte Historia*, which, he said
ironically, revealed the author's wide reading to more advantage
than his good judgment.

The section on judgment opened with a borrowing from
Vossius with which LeClerc agreed—that the good historian
would interpret indisputable facts in such a way that readers
would be both well informed and pleased. He said that in forming proper judgments, the historian must sort out the good topics
from the bad and must avoid those dealing with religious prefer-
ences. It was too easy to attribute victories to divine intercession,
as in the case of the Spanish historian Strade, who saw the favor
of God in every Spanish victory. Closer to home, LeClerc mentioned with contempt the works of Varillas and Maimbourg
"and other Liers [*sic*] of that stamp, who have renounced all
Truth" (p. 144). He posed the inevitable question: What sort
of Divinity should the good historian have in mind, and answered
that "he ought to consider God as the common Father of all
Mankind, who looks down with compassion upon their Errours
and their Vices, but contents himself with giving them Laws"
(p. 144) either to observe or to violate. The historian should
never attribute victory or defeat to divine justice or intervention.
In LeClerc's opinion, churchmen who flattered temporal powers
for personal advantage misused Divine Authority to blind readers
with the canard that the Christian religion was "an absolute
Empire over Men's Bodies and Souls" (p. 161).

The good historian had the duty to be a moralist and the
standard was, what LeClerc called, the "Principle of Humane
Society"; that is, the necessity of being just in human relations.
By his very impartiality, the good historian must condemn viola-
tors of this principle and praise its adherents. He said that
Plutarch had censured and praised but that his ideas of virtue
and vice were not compatible with modern ones because he had
made heroes out of warriors who, in reality, were "*Great
Scourges* both of their own Country and the neighbouring
Nations" (p. 148). LeClerc's own sense of impartiality led him
from Plutarch to writers of church history in whose works he saw

that virtue and vice had not been clearly separated in biographies of illustrious early Christians. He belabored the point that the Ancients had been honest in evaluating the moral aspects of their subjects but that modern historians too often dissembled. For an example he used Aubery's biography of Mazarin, where protection of his subject had created an erroneous picture of a man always good and pious.

LeClerc said that although Greek and Roman historians had surpassed the Moderns in freedom and accuracy of characterization, they had not always been impartial in their narratives. Both had praised warlike actions and had written without horror about the savagery and devastation of war; both had been so patriotic and so chauvinistic that they had never admitted the guilt nor the faults of their own nations. LeClerc attributed their blindness to narrow and limited ideas of justice and humanity. "They knew not that all Men are equal in matter of natural Right" (p. 151). On this basis, he asserted that Caesar had had no right to wage war against the Gauls and that Christians should not imitate pagans because Christianity taught that "all Men are Brothers ... by the Right of Nature proceeding from God" (p. 152). He queried, "By what Revelation do we know that God has given certain Rules of Justice to the Christians, and Laws altogether different to other People?" He had no ready answer and could only say, "For my part, I confess I don't know" (p. 153).

According to LeClerc, the problem of separating the true from false was made even more baffling by the absurdity that the *"Majority of Voices"* determined truth and that what the strongest believed was justice and the weakest, folly. This perversion of truth was more prevalent among Christian historians than among pagan ones. Thus, good ones had to have a strong sense of morality.

He said that even more was demanded. To the "Principle of Humane Society" and the need for morality, he must add a true understanding of politics because the chief end of politics and government was the bringing of "Happiness [to] those, whom God has committed to their [the rulers'] Care" (p. 157). He believed that happiness consisted in the people's obligation to obey the laws, in their right to enjoy both their estates and the fruits of their labors in tranquility and in their duty to contribute fair and equitable taxation for the maintenance of their society. If this definition was acceptable, the good historian had only to use it to arrive at proper judgments in matters of politics. There were no exceptions. Tyranny was to be condemned as were the pernicious ideas unfolded in Machiavelli's *The Prince*. The historian who championed tyranny was a slave.

English history provided LeClerc with an opportunity to defend British insistence on liberty. He said that these people would never be pawns for any king nor would they ever imitate the slavish ways of the French.[3]

He concluded this long essay with a paraphrase of Grotius's ideas of what nations owed each other and agreed that war should be condemned because it was "perfect Robbing and Murdering" (p. 164). In an astonishing display of passion, he appealed for an end to war and said that the historian must endorse the humanitarian principles against war fought solely to satisfy greed and ambition.

He recognized that he would antagonize those he had placed among the bad historians and that his strong plea for truth in history would not prevent flattery and lying, but he had had the satisfaction of asking them if they objected when one spoke the truth. His next essay, "Of the Decay of Humane Learning, and the Causes of it," was even more capable of bringing hostility of scholars and philologists to the surface.

In this essay, probably the most important in *Parrhasiana*, LeClerc looked closely at the state of affairs among philologists and what he saw was disheartening, to say the least. First, he exposed and then attacked their abuse of learning and warned of the consequences of continuation of it. What he said was very close to Swift's admirable chapters on the same subject in *A Tale of a Tub*. By different routes, both writers had arrived at the same conclusion: The state of learning was decaying and the fault lay at the door of those who were now the governors. LeClerc's essay became the target of attack in both Holland and England. Later, in his autobiography, he recalled that most of the essays had been received "by Men of an elegant Wit, and genteel Education, and Fortune," but that his views on the decay of learning had been attacked by "Those . . . who teach Human Learning in some Universities, and turn'd some Things against Him, contrary to his meaning; for what was said . . . where he Discourses of the Decay of the more elegant Letters, was truly and deservedly spoken against the Faults, and not the Men."

His explanation of this indignation was that he had touched very sensitive spots and had acted as an abrasive which had exposed what his decriers should have cured. "From that Time, some of those ... were ever after his greatest Enemies, and he found by Experience that they patronized the Faults, as well as the Persons. They persecuted him with virulent Calumnies, by which he gain'd only this; that it was plain that Mr. LE CLERC had spoken more Truth ... than was generally believ'd" (p. 34).

LeClerc had great faith in modern progress in philosophy and in science and believed that proper use of reason was routing superstition in religion and in natural philosophy. However, he was concerned about possible stagnation and decay in the commonwealth of learning. To give his essay sharp focus, he concentrated on the present condition of philology, an area of study with which he was very familiar. He saw with great clarity and with much sadness the steady decline in the number of illustrious scholars and critics; he looked back to the not very distant past when Europe had been blessed with such great scholars as Joseph Scaliger, Justus Lipsius, Isaac Casaubon, Claudius Salmasius, Hugo Grotius, John Meursius, and John Seldon, to name only a few of a remarkable and honorable list. But now there were none to equal them.

To account for the decline, LeClerc noted that few men were willing to dedicate their lives to humanity learning because of the attitude of established scholars who refused to encourage neophytes. He attacked those who maintained that because they got their knowledge "by a vast Reading and a prodigious Labour" (p. 167), they refused to make it less difficult for others. He said that learned men should do all possible to make the road to scholarly study less rocky and, as concrete evidence of their willingness to help younger men, should provide more accurate texts and editions of Latin and Greek writers and better books of all sorts.

Although LeClerc seemed to be addressing philologists associated with universities in Holland and in England, he was, at the same time, informing intelligent and curious readers that scholarship and learning were not the exclusive properties of the academic world. In his opinion, learning gained repute and usefulness when widely distributed—confining it to the university ghetto was to stifle it and to diminish its worth. Learning belonged to all.

To these ends he urged that scholars concentrate on writing notes and explications for difficult passages. He found that available editions were faulty because many scholars had insisted on expounding where the author had been clear and when the meaning had been "difficult and obscure, they [said] nothing" (p. 168). He charged them with the duty of presenting proper notes for those anxious to read the classics for pleasure and not "weary themselves in turning over large Volumes, to find the Explication of a Place they do not understand" (p. 169). This practical matter was best handled by writing short, authoritative notes, well worded and exact, to counteract prevalent notes full of quibbling or digression. He said that some remedial work was being done in Holland, where variorum editions were beginning to appear.

LeClerc pointed out that editions of Latin authors were superior to those of the Greek, where even the best qualified and learned men had not produced ideal ones. He found most translations only paraphrases, especially in difficult places, and said that the worst fault lay in those editions wherein the sense of the original was misrepresented because scholars were either ill-equipped, too easily discouraged, or too indolent. As an example of good Greek translation, he mentioned Isaac Casaubon's Polybius's histories and Theophrastus's *Characters.*

LeClerc brought into the open the pernicious attitude of exclusiveness by suggesting that good translations and illuminating notes were great helps to introduce the classics to an audience well beyond the ivory towers. He pleaded with "morose philologists" to rid themselves of their false belief that it was dangerous to make knowledge readily available for "Lazy Men," as they called all those not in their profession. He begged them to try to overcome their fears that learning would be less esteemed if widely spread. ". . . [W]hen a Science is useful and pleasant; the better it is known, the more it is cherished; and those, who know it, are so much the more esteem'd" (p. 175).

A second way he proposed which might halt the decay of learning was to provide good dictionaries like those by Henry Stephens and Robert Constantin, since, at present, there were only pitifully inadequate abridgments. Methodical treatises on the opinions and on the customs of the Greeks were needed to supply background material and to save interested readers much time and labor. But he stressed that more than methodical treatises and improvements in existing dictionaries, what was most urgently needed was a new dictionary or encyclopedia to supersede all the confusing and imperfect ones which hindered rather than helped provide clear information on the Ancients.

LeClerc next attacked pomposity and pride rampant among many humanists inclined to overpraise their own profession. Excessive claims and unearned praise had led to a breakdown of respect for the classics. He spoke out against many of his professional colleagues at home and abroad. "If you would believe them, they that never read [the classics], are not to be compared with those, that have. All other Sciences come not near this, which, they say, opens the way to all the Learning in the World" (p. 179). According to him, all this praise was questionable because, in the first place, the Moderns were just as valuable as the Ancients and, if the Ancients could have read the Moderns, they would have found them enlightening and instructive. Although refusing to meddle in the widespread dispute of the Moderns and the Ancients, he supported the argument that the moderns who were strangers to antiquity were not necessarily and automatically ignorant. He said that familiarity with the Ancients was valuable but that it was wrong to insist that classical works embodied all knowledge.

Secondly, he advised praising the Ancients with moderation and, as current practices of deception disappeared, readers would discover the greatness of the classics through their own efforts. After undercutting the pride inherent in overblown claims for the classics, he went a step further and helped destroy the groundless belief that classical learning could "soften ... Manners, and take away ... Wildness and Rusticity" (p. 181). Among classical scholars he found some who reasoned poorly and did not know how to arrange their thoughts in an orderly way; some who loaded their memories with many words but very few things; others who bit "every Body, [quarreled] with one another for Trifles, and [gave] one another the foulest Language" (p. 182). He announced that he could have written a whole volume on the subject of pedantry and pomposity among contemporary scholars and told them that if they were to live up to the praises and virtues which they claimed for the classics, they would help arrest the decay of humanity learning.

He turned to his third point and stated that there was little material support forthcoming from traditional sources—patrons,

Church, and State. He deplored the fact that neither Catholic nor Protestant universities offered sufficient posts to encourage humanity learning. In Catholic countries classical studies were undervalued and discouraged because of their uselessness in advancing either in church or in university. Even the Jesuits had such a low regard for humanity learning that they tolerated it only to train teachers of rhetoric. And, Catholic scholars were severely handicapped because they were forbidden to read the best Protestant critics. As for the Protestants, the case was different. Having to earn a living as preachers, they were forced to devote much time to preparing sermons and consequently had little left for scholarship.

He blamed Machiavellianism for much of this erosion because it defended ecclesiastical monarchy and the arbitrary power of temporal princes against ancient writings favoring more liberal ideas. Churchmen and statesmen, anxious to maintain their political power, were reluctant to support scholarship of no direct value to them.

Despite the decay that had set in, LeClerc was not ready to abandon humanity learning. It was beneficial everywhere as an instrument for bringing into communication all sorts of people with a wide variety of ideas. More importantly, it kept alive classical languages as "Interpreter[s], whom we carry along with us, to Travel . . . in an *Intelligible* World. . . . Without such . . . Interpreter[s], 'tis impossible to know what past [*sic*] in it" (p. 190).

The title of the next essay, "Of the Decay of some States," suggested political discussion, but LeClerc's design was not to write on politics but to examine in a general way the reasons why some nations fall into decay and he said that they did so because of reduction of population, undue burden of taxation, and internal discord. The situation in Spain supplied him with an opportunity to attack Catholicism in general and the devastation created by the multitude of priests, monks, and nuns who contributed nothing but consumed much. He accused them of hypocrisy by pretending that "the State [was] very much obliged to them" for instructing the people in religion and for saying that they were working very hard to implore "the Blessing of God, who never fails to hear their Prayers" (p. 194). He taunted that vows of celibacy were a force in keeping down population. As he put it, ". . . what they [the priests] boast of, may be done as well in the State of Marriage, and that they weaken their Country by not Marrying" (p. 194).

He showed that contrary to the case in Catholic countries, Holland, like ancient Rome, had gained much affluence through its hospitality to foreigners willing to settle there and through its care to keep its inhabitants prosperous and happy. "But they who founded that Common-wealth [Holland], seeing that many People faithful to the Government, under which they lived, were persecuted for their Religion ... resolved to receive all those, who would retire into their Country, provided they would obey the Civil-Laws" (p. 197). He said that Holland's heavy expenditures to alleviate the suffering of the poor exceeded the total revenue of some European States and that the Dutch policy of toleration was compatible with reason and revelation. It was so wise, admirable, and humanitarian that it fostered national pride and nourished industry for the benefit of the whole country.

After his commentary on the need for a happy, well-fed, burgeoning population, he took issue with the clergy and the nobility who, without industry, disclaim all responsibility for protecting and improving the State and only add their greed and extravagance to the burdens of responsible citizens. The privileged classes were composed of "useless Persons ... [who] trample on those, who can serve" the State (p. 203). Exorbitant taxation was closely allied to the problem of supporting official idleness, since the people were forced to sustain this virulent source of decay. To remove it, he said that the clergy and the nobility must either be curbed or be forced to repay what they had extracted from the nation.

He felt that national harmony was needed if a State were to flourish. People must agree on beneficial goals and work toward reaching them because internal dissension resulted when such generalities as concord, discord, union, and conspiracy were misunderstood. As an example he used "the Union of the *Inquisitors* in *Spain* and *Italy*, who perfectly agree ... to keep every Body in a profound Ignorance" (p. 213). This was union but, more importantly by its intention, a conspiracy against the people.

Religious persecution was cited as a chief source of decay. Only when toleration was accepted by all religions could a nation prosper. But LeClerc contended that such a condition would never exist because churchmen were always stirring up the people and politicians were always seizing on disturbances as opportunities to gain power. Amity and toleration exercised by both could lead to peace and tranquility. However, it would take men whose thoughts rose well above the common sort of self-interest to halt decay of the State.

The remaining essays in *Parrhasiana* were a motley collection. "A Vindication of Providence from the Objections of the Manichees" was a continuation of the old battle with Pierre Bayle. In it, LeClerc used Origen's arguments against the Manichees and their principles of the existence of evil and of divine indifference to the fate of Man. Admitting that moral and physical evils abound, he countered that Man could not complain because God did not require him to be without sin and did not condemn him for having sinned but for his not having repented. He also agreed with Origen's dictum that God did not act "by the limited and weak Notions of Men" (p. 221) because His ways were not Man's ways. At this point, LeClerc admitted that his treatment of the subject was incomplete but that he had written the essay for the sole purpose of inducing theologians to treat the matter more fully.

The essay "Men easily believe what their Passions suggest to them" was only an elaborate footnote to LeClerc's basic belief in the supremacy of reason over passion. He had discussed this issue many times and this repetition added nothing new. The entire essay was summed up in its title and in its opening sentence: "Men are apt to Believe what they Desire; and the weakest Reasons, which persuade 'em, appear to 'em like Demonstrations" (p. 226).

The next two sections like the preceding one were extremely brief. In "Of Praises and Censures" he argued that most praise was unmerited and only flattery. Often, it was a mask for ignorance. There were those who praised books they did not understand; there were those who praised books only because others did so. As for censure, it generally arose not from reasonable judgments but from envy and hatred and, therefore, these human failings had to be taken into account. He then pleaded that these remarks should be kept well in mind when reading history, especially ecclesiastical history, and that praise and censure should carry "no more Weight than Equity requires, and a severe Examination will allow" (p. 235). He warned against taking literally the epithets applied to bishops—"*most*

Holy," "most Pious," or "our most Holy *Father.*" At best they were only honorific and not descriptive; at worst they were flattery.

The essay "That it is a very difficult thing to Judge without Passion" could easily have been a continuation of the preceding one. He repeated his plea for use of reason and for distrust in passion when trying to make a judgment. He reiterated that passion hindered proper judgment and that when passion ceased, the "general Light of Reason and Equity . . . shines in our Minds" (p. 240). He said that the way to reduce it was through reflection and that he who never reflected was beyond recovery. He hoped in vain that religious zealots would be curbed but opposed them in an attempt to stem their proliferation.

The brief essays on praise and censure and on reason as opposed to passion were preludes to the final one, "Of Mr. LeClerc's Works," in which he reviewed what he had written up to 1700, describing and vindicating his numerous embroilments with critics in Holland, England, France, and Germany. Clearly, he had earned much fame as a controversialist throughout the republic of letters and, as his stormy career had developed he had become bolder, more positive, and more aggressive. Forerunner of a fuller account which was to appear in 1711, this essay was witness to the widespread interest and the heated responses he had generated. The quarrels, minutiae in the history of the times, are accurate barometers of his ability not only to disseminate ideas but also to arouse reactions which showed that he was dealing with topics of contemporary importance to scholars and to theologians in all parts of Western Europe.

Greatest attention was given Vander Waeyen, professor at Franeker, with whom he had had an uninterrupted battle for at least twenty years. Vander Waeyen had once called him a "Critico-Philosopher" and LeClerc now lectured him on the need for moderation and said that he could not understand excessive anger. If Vander Waeyen held contrary opinions, he should "refute . . . in a civil way" (p. 265). Anger was often associated with irrationality and LeClerc pitied those who used it instead of reason. Vander Waeyen had found fault with details in *Sentimens de Quelques Théologiens,* in *Five Letters,* in *Genesis,* in *Logic,* and elsewhere. LeClerc scoffed at the weak, critical comments and said that he had given up all hope of curing his

adversary of prejudice and of transgression of laws of charity
and of justice. Further, he urged Vander Waeyen to "forbear
writing Romances about other Men" (p. 268) unless he was content to have few people believe him. He contrasted Vander
Waeyen's odium and vituperation with Philip van Limborch's
well-tempered arguments and recalled that Van Limborch had
dealt with the accusation that LeClerc was a Socinian so expertly
as to "stop the mouth of any other Man but him" (p. 281).
LeClerc commented on Vander Waeyen's *Responsionis Limbor-
gianae Discussio* as a typical example of all his work. It is "a
confused heap of useless Quotations, and pitiful Arguments, without any Connexion, and Order, and sometimes the Reader is at
a loss to find any sense in it" (p. 281), and LeClerc added that
his opponent is so insensitive to reasonable arguments that he
never betrayed his "inward Shame."

LeClerc then referred briefly to his quarrels with Witsius,
professor at Utrecht; with Benoit, Minister at Delft; with Poiret,
the follower of Antoinette Bourignon; with Honcamp, canon
at Metz; with Maius, professor at Giessen; and with Etzard, professor at Wittenberg. But his exchanges with British churchmen,
with Dr. Kidder, Bishop of Bath and Wells, and Dr. Cave,
Canon of Windsor, are of special interest because in the case of
his differences with the British he displayed a moderate and, at
times, a respectful attitude, whereas with Continental critics
he was often blunt and intemperate. The reason appeared to be
his great respect and almost reverence for British thinkers and
for the British nation in general. He set "a greater value upon
the Judgment of that Free and Learned Nation, than upon all
the slavish and careless Divines of the rest of *Europe*" (p. 301).

The final section had in it at least two digressions of more than
passing interest. The first dealt with the use and abuse of conjecture; the second, with the famous Stillingfleet-Locke dispute
about the immortality of the soul. Digressions were rare in
LeClerc's work; he feared that the slightest movement away from
the main line of thought could lead to obscurity, but in these
cases his defense was that the miscellany was a genre in which
occasional informality was permissible.

In the first digression, a fine, brief, and complete essay, he
said that conjecture and reason were often confused. He used
his own work as an example and confessed that he had been
wrong in his remarks concerning the compiler of the *Pentateuch*.

The more complex a conjecture, the more danger it had because it was not grounded in truth. He complained that among the works of learned men conjecture had been all too prevalent even in those of so distinguished a scholar as Joseph Scaliger; he also made reference to an unnamed historian of great learning who was so full of conjectures built on conjectures of others that his arguments were "seldom cogent, and convince[d] few judicious and attentive Readers" (p. 258). In his opinion, the subject was so rich that a useful treatise should be written on it and he supplied an outline, dividing the topic into the following six parts: "1. Every Conjecture must be probable: 2. It ought to be as simple as possible: 3. No Consequences must be drawn from it: 4. One must speak of it doubtfully, as of a thing not certain: 5. No Body should think himself obliged in Honour to defend it, nor scruple to give it up: 6. He, who thinks himself obliged to maintain it, must not have recourse to new Suppositions" (p. 258).

The Stillingfleet-Locke dispute provided LeClerc with an opportunity to champion Locke and, perhaps, to fortify his reputation both in England and in Holland. The digression consisted mainly of a long excerpt from Locke's "Reply to the Bishop of Worcester's Answer to his Second Letter," which showed him at his best in rebuttal—in this instance, of the attack that he had lessened credibility in the immortality of the soul when he had argued that its immateriality could not be "demonstrated from natural Reason" (p. 275).

The rest of this section, devoted to a compilation of his works and with brief comments, was apparently intended to advertise them in the hope of advancing his ideas.

II   Parrhasiana, Part II

The quick success of *Parrhasiana* encouraged LeClerc and his Dutch bookseller, Henri Schelte, to undertake a sequel, which was published in 1701.[4] In the *avertissement,* he announced his satisfaction with Part I, both the French edition and the English translation, and hoped that the second would be as useful as the first. The second also followed the structure of the essay and he said that his chief aim was to be useful and if critics read anything else into his work, they would be going contrary to his intention and thought.

The first essay, *"Réflexions sur les Disputes des Gens de Lettres & particulièrement des Théologiens,"* revealed his continual preoccupation with disputatious matters, but he said that quarrels were valuable because they were an exciting way of testing veracity and of letting readers decide where truth lay. Besides, controversy made for lively reading, a factor not to be overlooked. One might question the propriety of witnessing men of letters, especially theologians, perpetually at war or, at least, at odds with one another, but he insisted that the search for truth was a moral obligation and that the method of attainment was secondary.

In the second essay, *"Pensées sur la nécessité & sur la manière d'étudier, pour les personnes qui ne font pas profession de Lettres,"* he developed the idea that even those who were unable to devote much time to study could learn to distinguish the true from the false and to appreciate good books. He claimed that there was no mystery in knowing how to judge truth or in how to see the validity of arguments leading to it. Borrowing heavily from Locke, he said that judicious people who had read the works of writers who had reasoned well and who could judge accurately from personal experiences, did not have to study rules of criticism. Common sense was the best road to travel in order to avoid error and to overcome prejudice.

He outlined methods for determining good works. There were three simple standards: First, the style must be clear and concise; second, the ordering of material must be logical and organic; third, the reasoning must be convincing. He found these rules satisfied in Tillotson's 52nd Sermon, in Grotius's *Du Droit de la Guerre & de la Paix*, in Pufendorf's *Du Devoir de l'Homme & du Citoyen*, and in Locke's *Essay Concerning Human Understanding*. In addition, he suggested the reading of the works of DeThou and Burnet because their histories were honest.

He said that if readers were confused, had no grasp of the material, or soon forget what they had read, the fault lay with the author and cited as examples *Les Essais de Morale*, from which nothing could be derived except a sense of stylistic elegance and a few isolated bits of thoughts; and the histories of Maimbourg and Varillas, which were inexact and filled with flattery.

He told readers to forget any notions they might have of the hard work which good reading entailed and even encouraged them to reread good books. If they complained that so much application was beyond their capabilities, he sternly countered that study was not a game but a serious enterprise well worth the effort to elevate them above those easily hoodwinked by specious arguments, blinded by ignorance, and frustrated by injustice. He added that they needed to master Latin, French, and especially English in order to read *belles lettres* in the original and to avoid the dangers inherent in bad translation, since thoughts cast in poetic language, good in the original, often became ludicrous in translation which destroyed cadence, altered word order, and used approximate synonyms.

The third essay, "*Moyens de rendre une République heureuse,*" was a general compilation of current ideas derived from the popular cult of happiness which was to become so dominant in British thinking later in the eighteenth century. LeClerc called attention to Locke's *An Essay Concerning the true Original Use of Civil Government,* which had dealt well with the subject, mentioned that it was available in England but, more importantly, that it was now to be had in Amsterdam in French translation. It was clear from this reference how important he believed Locke's work to be and that he deemed it necessary to increase its popularity on the Continent, especially in Holland.

Essentially, LeClerc was not a political man and, therefore, he simply restated the ideas of Locke. He, too, saw clearly that education was the basis of good laws under which a nation could find happiness and suggested that it would be very useful if there were established professors "*du Droit de la Nature & des Gens*" to equal the vast number of those in other sciences— that these teachers could do much to train youth for useful participation in government by exposing them to good examples from ancient and modern history. They could introduce many books to their students on the ideas of justice, equity, and order and, thereby, would promote public tranquility and would preserve good laws and liberty. He pointed out that as a result of such learning, eventually, people would demand and get better government. Widespread citizen participation was necessary to safeguard not only civil but also ecclesiastical government. Following the general lines of latitudinarianism, he advocated constant vigilance to prevent formation of a tyrannical system. He cited the unsettled state in England from Cromwell to William III and praised the Glorious Revolution which, in his opinion, was a good example where revolution had established liberty with just laws and had resulted in a good King and in an active Parliament. In a rare adverse comment on England, LeClerc anticipated Rymer's *Foedera* by pointing out that British laws and acts of Parliament were often ambiguous and very difficult to clarify and supported Edmund Ludlow's similar observation that this situation needed correction.

This is also what I do, with all my heart, in regard to all the Greater and Lesser Powers and especially those which the United Provinces, and the Power of Holland in particular, obey. May they safeguard eternally all that is truly useful for them and their peoples, and correct all that might be harmful for them; so that their Republic, their Provinces and their Towns may be Schools of Good Sense and Virtue, and Models of the happiest State that one can imagine on this Earth!   (pp. 309-310, translated)

III   Five Letters Concerning the Inspiration of the Holy Scriptures

From the very beginning of his career, LeClerc sought truth through good reasoning more than through inspiration and said that revelation was reserved for those true mysteries which the Divine had elected to keep beyond human comprehension. As he pursued his search, he pointed out faults no matter where they appeared and by so doing tried to dispel obscurity.

His ability to provoke response is a valuable gauge of the impact of his ideas; his works were so inflammatory that they drew long replies from some of the most eminent theologians in England. Such engagements were commonplace; public debate and discussion were acceptable and vital in a period when orthodox opinions and traditional interpretations were being brought under the attack of thinkers like Locke and publicists and theologians like LeClerc.

Later, in his autobiography, he made some general comments on the attacks and said that he had been indifferent to his critics since he had been "very willing and ready to embrace the Truth, from whatever Quarter it should happen to shine." He said that he had welcomed attacks hoping that in them he might find truth. But, although his magnanimity and toleration appear reasonable, he had been more ready to defend his position than to accept those of his critics. At a distance of almost three centuries, LeClerc's opinions on inspiration of the sacred writers seem quiet and even pedestrian, but in his own time they were disturbing and disruptive to the British who held conservative views in theological matters.

When he attacked Father Simon's *Critical History of the Old Testament* in *Sentimens de Quelques Théologiens de Hollande,* he included in Letters XI and XII a small treatise, *Five Letters Concerning the Inspiration of the Holy Scriptures,* and stated that his chief purpose was "only to engage Learned Men to write on that Subject."[5] He could not possibly have realized how provocative his treatise would become and how eagerly learned British divines would take issue.

Naturally, the first strong objection came from Father Simon. LeClerc said that the reply had "all the Passion and Animosity, that could be expected from a Man, who could alledge [*sic*] no good Reason; and ... used all the injurious and unbecoming Words that he could think of, on such an occasion."[6] He corrected Father Simon's error in thinking that Pierre Allix and Aubert de Versé were the authors of the treatise.

LeClerc chose to brush aside without much comment the attacks by Matthias Honcamp, canon at Metz, and Joannes Henricus Maius, professor at Giessen. He said that the former deserved to be treated sharply but that the latter was more dangerous for what he taught his students in Germany than for his ill-tempered and poorly reasoned critical remarks. His consistent contempt for these German theologians and professors was the same he meted out to his countryman, Joannes Vander Waeyen, who, following Maius and Honcamp, believed that Aubert de Versé was the author of *Five Letters.* LeClerc corrected him, made it clear that this work had been written by someone designated only by the letter *N,* and challenged him to prove De Versé's authorship.

LeClerc's commentary on his critics is of limited significance but it establishes the fact that *Five Letters* was widely read in England, in France, in Germany, and in Holland. When it first came out in 1685, English critics had been remarkably silent but after it had appeared in translation in 1690, British churchmen expressed their opposition. It is clear that his widening reputation in England depended heavily on translated publication because British theologians neither read foreign publications nor had them readily available.

Before undertaking to present the vehement opposition to *Five Letters* in England, it may be appropriate to outline the essential, provocative material in it. In the preface, the translator carefully set the background by telling readers the provenance of the treatise and by describing Father Simon's book as a Roman tract, saying that it had "raised him many Antagonists amongst the Protestants beyond the Seas." He stated further that *Five Letters* was among the swiftest replies to Father Simon and praised its author who "appears second to none, either in Critical Learning, or Solid Judgment." He went on to note that the author "propounds a middle way, which he conceived proper to settle in Men's Minds a just esteem of the Scriptures, upon a solid Foundation." This elaboration was necessary because, evidently, LeClerc's work was not yet sufficiently well known and, more importantly, the British were still not fully conversant with Father Simon's book despite the publicity given it in Dryden's *Religio Laici*.

Briefly, LeClerc presented a series of letters in which he probed the possibility that ecclesiastical history would be true only when reexamined in the clear light of reason. Letter I attacked the use of inspiration in writing history and argued that truth derived from factual sources and from right reason should be the bases for all kinds of histories. Letter II doubted the inspirational qualities generally attributed to the Apostles. Letter III satirized Father Simon as "that incomparable Critic," presented a detailed commentary on the irresponsibility of modern critics, an argument against the imputation that LeClerc was a deist, and a defense for the good name of Grotius. Letter IV systematically answered objections which Father Simon had raised. Letter V consisted of a longer rebuttal against the allegation of deism.[7]

After the translation had received wide circulation among British churchmen, LeClerc was attacked by Claude Grosteste Lamothe, Dr. John Williams, William Lowth, and others. Lamothe called it a work injurious to the Scriptures and likely to have evil consequences.[8] He said that he was a member of a large group writing in opposition and that he had read the replies of Witsius in Holland, of Lowth in England, and of Simon in France. But his treatise was less an argument against LeClerc's opposition to inspiration and more a warning against his position. He treated LeClerc as a promoter of evil and as a deceiver rather than as an intellectual adversary in theological discussion. "I know nobody that has more formally assail'd the Inspiration of the Sacred Books of the New Testament. *Spinoza* led the way.... But M. N. [LeClerc] has given a more subtle and more dangerous Air to *Spinoza's* Notions and has digested them into a System." He said that he had learned from a friend of LeClerc's that this treatise "has been look'd upon by several, as a Step that leads directly to *Deism*; and the Author [LeClerc] likewise is accus'd of favouring that abominable Opinion" (p. 12). The only semblance of effective rebuttal appeared in his observation that when LeClerc had pulled Father Simon's book to pieces, he had reduced its value. A book, said Lamothe, was "only esteemed for the happy Assemblage of Words and Things of what it is compos'd: After you have destroy'd the Proportion and the Symmetry, you will no longer find what caus'd it to be admir'd" (p. 63).

Williams, Chaplain in Ordinary to his Majesty, preached seven sermons at St. Martin's-in-the-Fields during 1695, in the sixth of which he touched on this treatise. His was a modest and quiet defense entitled "The Divine Authority of the Scriptures."

Lowth, Chaplain to the Lord Bishop of Winchester, called attention to Lamothe's treatise and to Williams's sermon and, in the prefatory address, complained that "It is the Misfortune of our times to have Religion at once assaulted by a Rude and Ignorant Profaneness [*sic*], by a Confident potence [*sic*] to reason, and by Sceptical Sophistry."[9] His reply was couched more in terms of fear than in those of confident argument. He saw LeClerc as one "to Perplex Men's minds with Difficulties... and ... render the Divine Authority of those Writings suspected...." He believed that LeClerc was not only a Spinozist but what was worse, an improver on Spinoza. Then he attacked him for his alleged Socinianism and described the treatise as "no better than Preaching another Gospel, and believing in another Jesus" (p. 6). Lowth's book was an attempt to answer LeClerc's argument against divine inspiration of the Scriptures but it harbored more passion than reason and, when frustrated, he moved from LeClerc to the anonymous translator, who had acknowledged that "this Treatise is not Calculated for the use of simple-hearted Pious persons," and asked, "If not for these then were they translated for 'Dishonest, Illiterate Atheists'?" (p. 249).

While these three examples show English interest in LeClerc's ideas, they are only the surface manifestation of the depth of penetration and the longevity of his work among the British. Ten years after *Five Letters* had appeared it was still being discussed. Edmund Calamy preached a series of sermons between August 22, 1704, and June 11, 1706, on the subject of inspiration of the holy writings and, apparently, these were thought topical enough to be printed as late as 1710. He recalled that "the anonymous Author of the Five Letters ... has been already answer'd by several," yet he felt that LeClerc's subtlety and artifice were still dangerous enough to infect the unwary with deistic and Socinian ways. In the first sermon, Calamy tried to refute LeClerc's so-called dangerous utterances and in the second he attacked LeClerc's statement that a man does not need inspiration to relate faithfully what he has seen. In the third, he disagreed with LeClerc's observation that "St. Luke learn'd not that which he told us by Inspiration, but by Information from those who knew it." In the fourth, he challenged that there was no passage in the Gospel where Christ said that all the books in the Old Testament were divinely inspired. In later sermons, he undertook to expose the falsity he saw in the provocative statement: "The Apostles did not pass in their own time for Persons, every word of whose was an Oracle."

Calamy's steady plodding through *Five Lett*ers was by far the best contemporary, orthodox presentation. Yet it failed to capture the attention accorded Lowth's earlier pamphlet, which had gone through editions in 1692 and in 1699 and, as late as 1821, had appeared in a third, where an advertisement explained that it was printed "to meet the demand among Theological Readers."[10]

LeClerc's *Five Letters*, the response to the English translation, and the longevity of both were good indications of steady interest in the controversy over inspiration. The core of LeClerc's argument was his belief that those who recorded the events in the New Testament were only reporters and that as historians they must be viewed without any recourse beyond the human. To confuse historical writings with inspirational ones led to distortions and misunderstandings which, in turn, caused confusion and incredulity. Understandably, his opponents in England could see the consequences arising from acceptance of the sacred writings as profane ones and tried valiantly to maintain their orthodox position which, in the minds of men like Locke, Shaftesbury, Van Limborch, and LeClerc, was completely untenable.

IV The Causes of Incredulity

LeClerc looked beyond his argument against the inspirational qualities in the sacred writers and recognized that if inspiration was acceptable then the reasonableness of Christianity would become suspect. The inevitable conclusion was the necessity to examine the actual and potential causes of incredulity and he found it expedient to write *The Causes of Incredulity*, which appeared in English translation in 1697. This topic was of great importance, he said, because until now "no one had with sufficient Accuracy taught what it was, which deterr'd the Incredulous"[11] from accepting Christianity. His argument hinged on examination of the causes of incredulity found in man and his environment. He charged churchmen with the responsibility of routing it and said that for his part, his design was to try to convince doubters that they no longer had reason to refuse acceptance of Christian doctrine and to encourage believers not to be swayed by trifles.

In *Parrhasiana* (Part I) he said that this treatise explained that "the better a Man reasons, the better he may be convinced of the Truth of the Christian Religion . . . and that Men fall into Unbelief for want of reasoning well." Without "the Light of Reason, we can apprehend nothing in Revelation" and, as he had argued before, its "necessary Obscurity" was not the same as contradiction because the latter could not be found in truth. He said that there are some mysteries which men can never penetrate but they are still true. Christians should accept and not try to explain them; "Reason teaches us that God created the World out of nothing, but no Man can know the manner of it."[12]

The treatise was quickly translated and enjoyed a wide range of influence. The translator said that the author was a "Person so well known to all the learned World, that it could not be thought less arrogant than superfluous . . . to give any Character of his Capacity or his Writings." In addition, he revealed that LeClerc had leaned heavily on Grotius but had improved on him. While Grotius was intelligible to scholars, LeClerc was clear to all men. Thus, the translator was in tune with LeClerc's steady efforts to clarify and to simplify complicated material and to eradicate the fallacy that only the learned had the privilege and the capacity to understand the grounds of their religion.

In his study LeClerc found at least five reasons to account for incredulity in religion: pride; prejudice; lack of knowledge on how to reason well; neglect of searching into truth; and laziness. He urged the use of common sense and asked only that the unbeliever listen to reason. The temper of the treatise was evident in the conclusion to the first part, where he asserted, "It is . . . infinitely more reasonable and more sure both for this and the other Life, if there be one, to search after Truth, and to examine the Proofs of Religion, than to live and die in the most extravagant Carelessness imaginable. . . . This examination is of the utmost Importance, there is nothing to be lost by making of it, and you risk all by neglecting it."

Here, LeClerc expressed as clearly as possible his reliance and his insistence on the power of reason to strip away unexamined traditions, to expose shaky foundations and to establish truth. He said that objective investigation must not be confined to natural philosophy alone, but that it was also serviceable in other areas where truth was often hidden by mythology, panegyrics, and blind acceptance of old authority.

He insisted that this treatise was so convincing that "no reasonable Man can oppose" it. Yet Vander Waeyan had attacked it on the specious grounds that it had denied the existence of "true Mysteries." In reply, LeClerc admitted that "he [was] no great Admirer of the Mystical Explications of Prophecies; which [Vander Waeyan gives] to us."[13] With restraint, LeClerc said that he was content to let the Cocceians and others of their ilk enjoy their great ignorance but that they should not object when the more enlightened preferred to meditate on the lessons of the Gospel and to grow to love its precepts.

Another objection came from Dr. Cave, biographer of the Primitive Fathers, who had taken exception to the observation that some divines "dishonour Religion by their scandalous Lives." LeClerc referred readers to the treatise itself, where he had argued that churchmen who lead vicious lives contribute to incredulity. In defense, he said that those who exposed hypocrisy were, in reality, friends of the churchmen because exposure could lead to reform for them. His argument was summed up in the following passage:

... those, who cannot abide that such Men should be censured, and who omit nothing to palliate, and consequently to perpetuate their Faults, which the People imitate or abhor, and which give occasion to Unbelievers to reject the Christian Religion, those, I say, are truly Enemies to Christian Divines and Religion, and only Friends to *Church-Preferments* and *Ecclesiastical Authority*.[14]

V The Lives of the Primitive Fathers

In *The Causes of Incredulity*, the direction of LeClerc's thinking had been set by Descartes and by Locke, but he took a step beyond them when he wrote *The Lives of the Primitive Fathers*. He had written at length against the use of panegyric in ecclesiastical history in *Bibliothèque Universelle et Historique* and, in 1701, these pieces were collected and translated into English.[15] In the preface, the translator established that LeClerc had written for a wide, general public and that in England he was "well-known by his Writings."

LeClerc examined the works of Clemens and of Gregory and because of their bad style, found them obscure in dealing with difficult matters. Clemens, he said, was harsh and pompous and these flaws had led to lack of order which weakened solid proofs because the "Author confounds himself, ... and heaps up an infinite number of Arguments which prove nothing."[16] As for Gregory's writings, they were "too full of Figures"—a good breeding ground for obscurity; and, his "Thoughts [were] heaped one upon another, as they came into [his] Mind."[17] Expanding his commentary on the dangers inherent in bad style and addressing himself to contemporary divines in Holland and in England, he wrote, "... those who have an Obscure Style, have no clear Head; and ... they speak so, because they do not apprehend things more clearly than they speak 'em."[18] While he agreed that there were occasions to use ornaments in prose, clarity was more important and should never be sacrificed for the sake of "fancy writing."

He accused Dr. Cave of dishonesty because he glossed over defects which could not be hidden behind the façade of truth and rebuked him for his observation that Clemens and Gregory should be commended "for their clearness and perspicuity, their

eloquent stile [*sic*] and grave Discources [*sic*]." In an acri-
monious exchange, Dr. Cave charged that LeClerc was "ill
affected to *Christian Divines*" and LeClerc replied in his standard
fashion that exposure of flaws in the characters of churchmen
was not a crime; it was, instead, a good thing to halt perpetuation
of their faults.[19]

In his autobiography, LeClerc said that the subject raised in
The Lives of the Primitive Fathers could not be readily dismissed. Ecclesiastical history must be honest; otherwise, it
degenerated into flattery and ultimately turned misinformation
into pseudo-truth. The whole purpose of *The Lives*, he said;
was to guard against the "gross Flatteries of Panegyrists" which
"were rather Reproaches and Lies than true Commendations."
The eulogists "indulge their Passion, rather than follow the
perfect Light of Right Reason."[20]

VI Reflections upon what the World Commonly Call Good-Luck and Ill-Luck

Falsehoods growing out of flattery were very close to superstition, and for men of LeClerc's temper superstition was the
fiercest enemy of truth. He fought it wherever he could and
eagerly did so in a typical work, *Reflections upon ... Good-Luck
and Ill-Luck*, which rapidly found its way to England by way
of translation.[21] Friends had persuaded him to elaborate on
his views, since "such a Tract could not cost [him] any great
Pains; and that a few Days would suffice for putting [his]
Thoughts into Writing." He "resolved to let the World see,
both [his] own Reasons, and the Objections they are liable to."[22]

His purpose was not to criticize lotteries but simply to explore
the subject reasonably. The appearance of his work coincided
with the mania for lotteries already firmly established in England
and gaining quick acceptance in Holland. In 1694 a British
lottery had raised a million pounds sterling and the Dutch
were anxious to join the game. LeClerc saw that the Dutch
were "as greedy of advancing Mony [*sic*], as if they lent it at
a large Interest.... All Holland being now warm in these
Projections."[23]

Superstition in religion had always been under his attack,
but in this work LeClerc moved into the secular milieu where
he found an alarming situation. He used lotteries and gambling

as a topical excuse to attack superstition. In the preface he
described it as "A Disease exceeding common, bred up and
cherished by early Prejudices; and though incident chiefly to
weak Minds, yet very rarely rooted out entirely by the strongest."
He continued, "One cannot, without Indignation, hear Persons,
who profess to Believe and Understand the Gospels, laying a
Stress upon *Fatal Numbers, Climacterical Years, Childermass
Days, Lucky Hours, Successful Physicians,* and a Hundred other
such senseless Trifles."

His commentary followed the well-worn path of those who
had decried the confusion arising from confounding words with
things. Catch phrases as "Good Luck" and "Ill Luck" had, in
reality, neither "Sense nor Signification." Fortune was only a
word and he wondered, "How can you do anything with it?"
In the same class was destiny. Prime abusers of such senseless,
fuzzy words were writers whose prose or poetry would lose
"its fairest Flowers, if *Destiny* and *Fortune* were no more."[24]
He recognized the seduction these words carried and realized
the difficulty of giving them up. But he distrusted verbal ornamentation because "These and other Words of like Importance
carry Musick in the Sound, they strike the Ear, and help Rhyme
at a dead lift, so seasonably, so agreeably, that though never
so offensive to Reason, parted with they must not be upon any
Terms. And all this is owing to Custom."[25] For support he called
upon La Fontaine's *Fables,* in which, borrowing from the Dutch
writer Van Dale, La Fontaine had said, "The Good is all our
own, the Ill is Fortune's." And LeClerc, extending this maxim,
debunked the commonly held notion that one's good angels
procure money.

LeClerc was not against lotteries but against their abuse. He
suggested that the money raised be used not for armaments
but for relief of the poor. In this way a case could be made
endowing the lottery with morality. He saw this game of chance
as a developer of greed because tickets were bought solely
for covetous gain, but if public benefit could be instituted, the
stigma would be mitigated. He further suggested, rather whim-
sically, that worthy benefactors could be men of learning.
Francis Bacon had suffered poverty while James I had advanced
worthless men and, using himself, perhaps, as an example, he
argued in behalf of scholars who could no longer find patrons.

At present the improvement of Learning, the study of Sacred and Profane Antiquity, skill in Languages, a nice Taste and sound Judgment, zealous love of Truth, a moderate and peaceable Temper, wasting a Man's self with perpetual toil for the Instruction of Mankind; These are Qualities that turn to little account else, than merely the attracting of Envy, or the getting some little cold Recommendation.[26]

He observed that money was good but that education was better. Following Locke, he admonished parents to save for the good education of their children and not to try to leave them wealth derived from lotteries or fortune or good luck. "It is much better and kinder, to leave them less in Mony [*sic*], provided they be rich in good Sense, and good Principles; for without those Qualifications, an Estate does more hurt than good."[27]

The treatise was for the ever-serious LeClerc a fanciful work written, he said, as a diversion. What he advocated made good sense and good moralizing, but its greatest impact appeared to be in its inadvertent warning that when pressed too far, these precepts could lead to practical absurdity; they could not combat human greed and covetousness. He knew that his exhortation to use the monies for the poor and for scholars would be futile because the unthinking would always remain heedless, yet he tried to make his argument convincing.

The writings described in this chapter were part of LeClerc's fight against superstition, pedantry, obscurantism, and greed. In each case he offered a practical solution. Superstition could be extirpated by facts; pedantry, eliminated by absolute honesty; obscurantism, unmasked by simplicity of expression; greed, crushed by morality. His handling of these subjects was in harmony with the beliefs held by the advanced thinkers of his day and, as a result, his publications were valuable contributions to the dissemination and to the growth of those ideas that eventually found favor in the later decades of the eighteenth century.

VII *Editions of Grotius and Erasmus*

The search for truth followed many paths but for LeClerc the three main ones were humanity learning, philosophy, and divinity. The ideal was to combine them in order to create a high and wide road on which all men could travel. Grotius and Erasmus had been among the pioneers in this important endeavor, and when occasion arose LeClerc praised their works and used them to support his own. Even though both were well known throughout the republic of letters before LeClerc's time, as a publicist and as a man of learning, he was impelled to do all he could to make their works more readily available and better understood. He knew that they were more talked about than read and, to reverse this all too common situation, he became their editor, translator, commentator, and champion. To LeClerc, both men were, indeed, incomparable.

In praise of Grotius, he could say nothing more than that he had the great talent to bring together these three chief disciplines. Lamenting that in his own day "... Things, which should be inseparable, are now divided," he recalled earlier times when "the Famous *Hugo Grotius,* whose Writings are above Envy, joyned together the three Sciences."[28] But in the spirit of an enlightened Modern, LeClerc believed that the art of thinking had been so refined and developed that even Grotius could be surpassed as reason became better used, and he envisioned the tremendous potentialities of his own age. "Suppose," he wrote, "there were now in *Holland,* many such Men as *Grotius,* or more Learned than he was, (a thing not impossible, if Men studied as they should) how great an influence would their Learning have, not only in the *United Provinces,* but also over all *Europe!*"[29]

LeClerc's editions and translations of Grotius's major works contributed to the advancement of his reputation; he brought them before an audience well beyond the restricted limits of the learned world. An edition of *The Truth of the Christian Religion* appeared in 1709 and new ones followed in a steady procession for more than a century.[30] Proud of his work, LeClerc referred to it as a "very fair Edition of those Golden Books" and added that he always carried with him something Grotius had written.[31]

The affinity with Grotius was not based on complete intellectual agreement. For example, LeClerc added an essay to his edition in which he questioned the statement about which society of Christians one ought to join. He argued that a man ought to join that group which imposed nothing beyond a belief in the "unquestionable Memorials of Divine Revelation, to be the

Doctrine of our Saviour."[32] But, between them was community of spirit in application of common sense, in honesty of expression, and in sincerity in the search for truth. As a result, LeClerc could comfortably follow Grotius's methodology without succumbing to intellectual slavery. Perhaps he saw himself as a latter-day Grotius who suffered needlessly because he chose to follow reason and moderation. This kindred relationship was attested to when he remarked, "it far'd with HUGO GROTIUS before, as it does with [mc] now, and the Objections thrown against [us], hurt one, as well as the other."[33]

In LeClerc's opinion, the only Dutch writer to equal Grotius was Erasmus, and he brought out an edition of his works in ten volumes. The first appeared in 1703; the final ones, in 1706. This edition, LeClerc said, was the finest ever produced by Peter Vander Aa, the Leyden bookseller noted for the excellence of his printing.

LeClerc believed that the great merit in Erasmus's work as in that of Grotius was the integration of humanity learning, philosophy, and divinity and, once again, he regretted modern fragmentation of these disciplines. Now philologists insisted that their own branch of learning embraced all sense and that some divines "measure every Thing by their Cobweb-Distinctions ... and are not able to Expound or Read the Holy Scriptures."[34] He praised Erasmus for his theological works and noted especially the translation of the New Testament and the commentaries on the Epistles. He said that Erasmus had infused new life into "the Queen of all Sciences, Theology" by the widest possible range of scholarship and by the strength of his "Sagacity, and Probity of Mind." Through his work Erasmus proved that he "well knew, that True Religion ... [consisted] in stirring us up with the Love of God and our Neighbor."[35] LeClerc found the *Colloquies* especially noteworthy and said that while they had been read and admired, Erasmus had been forced to write apologies for them.

He believed that in his role as editor, his greatest contribution lay in his handling of the epistles; he had determined their proper sequence and, through accurate chronology, had been able to remove much of the confusion in earlier editions.[36] Correction of a few details was not an attempt to appear superior but was necessary because Erasmus had often been wrong "when he was deceiv'd by the deprav'd Lections of bad Editions;

He sometimes nodded too, which is granted on all Hands in such a multiplicity of Writing."[37] As for detractors and petty critics, LeClerc said that these could be endured easily since Erasmus's work rose high above them.

His respect for Erasmus is evident in the panegyric in the autobiography; it is a small masterpiece of critical appraisal to present the true spirit of his countryman. LeClerc tempered his praise by recalling that Erasmus "us'd a sharp Pen against... some impertinent and idle Wretches, and that when he perceiv'd his *Reputation* struck at, ... put on Iron Gloves."[38] He justified Erasmus's vehemence in attacking detractors in this query: "Who can be angry at a Man, who was surrounded with violent and almost daily Contentions... [and] was forc'd to return their Indignation upon them who drew against him without Provocation?" Notwithstanding, he found that Erasmus had an "amiable, jocose, and pleasant Temper, ... and by Jocularity rather than by biting Sarcasms gain[ed] over his Adversaries to a juster Opinion of him."[39]

In his biography of Erasmus, John Jortin wrote that he had been so impressed with LeClerc's judgments that he confessed his inability to do better and quoted the entire section from the autobiography. He said, "I found his way of thinking and judging... correspondent with mine; and I have seldom had occasion to declare a dissent from him.... I pay my grateful acknowledgements to him once for all. His labours and mine are blended together; and I am persuaded that his Manes, if the Deceased concern themselves about such things, will not be offended at the use which is here made of his work."[40] As for the corrections, Jortin said, "LeClerc often censures Erasmus for his luke-warmness, timidity, and unfairness, in the matter of the Reformation; and I ... have adopted these censures, only softening them a little here and there; for I am, in the main, of the same opinion... as to this point."

In *Reflections upon Learning*, printed in London in 1699, Thomas Baker attacked LeClerc for citing faults in Erasmus and said, "I have treated all Men with Decency and Respect, except Mons. LeClerc, who has not deserv'd such Treatment." In examining the state of learning, Baker found that modern critics had degenerated into mere grammarians and used LeClerc as an example. He complained that "Monsieur LeClerc, is as free in his Censures, as any Man I ever met with, and oft times as Unhappy."[41] And, when Robert Masters wrote his memoirs of Thomas Baker, he approved of the censure of LeClerc but was not content with perpetuating Baker's judgment of him. He had read Jortin's biography and said that Baker had "attacked LeClerc with a Virulence which one would not have expected from a Man, who, as I remember, was accounted ... a candid, genteel and polite Person." But in the end, Masters concluded that Baker was a "Man of the strictest Veracity" and that LeClerc's was questionable.[42]

LeClerc's greater enthusiasm was for Erasmus rather than for Grotius. As a theologian, he could more readily and more fully understand the mind of Erasmus whereas his interests were often removed from Grotius's discussions of politics, war, and international justice. In a sweeping generality which encompassed the predicament of these two great men and himself, LeClerc observed that the condition of "Learned Men and Learning" was the same in all ages. The actors were different but the drama was always the same. "In former Times," he said, "there were Persons very instrumental for the Good of the Republic of Letters; there were likewise several who endeavour'd to obscure and detract from their Merit. The same Persons are now, and such there will be for ever."[43]

VIII *Biblical Studies*

In the complicated and turbulent world of theology, LeClerc was a leader among those who saw the need for a scientific approach to the Old and New Testament. Uncritical praise, careless reliance on tradition, and folly in hiding ignorance in silence were no longer valid. He brought the full force of his critical energies to bear on his translations of the Bible, on his attempts to find harmony in Christianity based on reason, and on his exegesis but, most of all, he looked forward to the day when biblical scholarship would become dispassionate and when reason would replace centuries-old passion, bias, and prejudice. In *Parrhasiana* he had described the problems in writing history and now he followed his own precepts. His goal was "the Dilucidation, Exposition and Defence of the Truth and Virtue."[44]

His periodicals, many treatises, miscellanies, and commentaries were studded with biblical references and all of them became parts of the background for his theological works. In 1684 he

had worked on a Latin translation of the Old Testament but
with so many projects interposed, he had had to postpone its
completion until 1693. In spite of his familiarity with the
subject and his fearlessness, he began the project cautiously.
He recognized that a scientific approach might lead to needless
bickering and might be unacceptable even to modern scholars.
Accordingly, in 1690, he circulated among friends in England
and in Holland a single leaf in quarto containing a paraphrase
and commentary on the prophet Obadiah and asked for their
opinions. Graevius, not yet his enemy, wrote from Utrecht in
December, 1690, that the specimen had been well received
there and that readers were eager to have more; it was "a
noble Enterprize."

Another correspondent was Bishop Burnet. "Your works are
as highly valued by some as they are censured by others. Indeed
this on the Bible is invaluable." After reflecting on the lack of
popular support for such great efforts, Burnet offered some
suggestions on the projected study. "When you come to the
Psalms I hope you will not insist too much on the Essay you
once gave of the Rythms [sic] in it for that will make strange
transcriptions. I am sure one observation will not scape [sic]
you that the Psalms being sung by the Scribes in turns and
sometimes with single voices, sometimes by a Chorus. This gives
a beautiful account of many repetitions and of the changes
both of the person from the first to third and of the number from
the singular to the Plural." He also advised LeClerc to set aside
temporarily at least his firm opinion that *Job* was an epic and
that the *Songs of Solomon* was a pastoral and to entertain
other possible readings.[45]

Satisfied with the response, LeClerc "willingly undertook that
Work, . . . because he always took great delight in that Study,"[46]
and in 1693 he brought out the commentary on *Genesis*. In 1695
a commentary on the whole of the *Pentateuch* appeared and,
at about the same time, a study of the beginning of *St. John's
Gospel* was published.

Among British divines who had commented was Richard
Kidder, Bishop of Bath and Wells, who had carried on a long
correspondence with LeClerc on his paraphrase of the *Pentateuch*. This exchange of letters had started as far back as
November 9, 1694, but LeClerc had kept it private until 1704,
when he printed three of them in *Bibliothèque Choisie*, Tome

IV, and justified publication on the grounds that Kidder was now dead and could not be harmed. Kidder had made derogatory remarks but had agreed to give LeClerc full satisfaction in a forthcoming publication and, at the same time, had told him that he now believed the paraphrase of the *Pentateuch* to be a work "excelling anything the world yet had of that kind." According to LeClerc, the dispute had been based not on a wide difference of opinion but on a deception practiced by an unnamed British critic who had tricked Kidder into writing against him.[47]

In keeping with his principle of making subject matter intelligible to laymen, he kept the texts free from controversy, inquiring only into literal sense and meaning. His general method involved looking at the Old Testament "as if he had been the first, who undertook such a Work." For example, he considered the meaning inherent in the word testament, suggesting that it must be understood in a metaphorical sense because it was a legal term used exclusively among men. He observed that metaphorical terms were dangerous because they were "seldom grounded upon a perfect Similitude between those things, to which they are indifferently applied; and therefore they cannot always be scrued [sic] up to the whole Latitude of their natural signification."[48] He clarified and reinforced his argument on the weakness of words by stating that doubt must be confessed and not be transformed into something vague, as if it were certain and established. Wise men refrained from expressing certainty where there was doubt. He noted that this principle was not easy to follow because many "love to conceal their Ignorance, and had rather seem learned than really be so."

Two more works appeared in rapid succession. LeClerc had started working on a translation and commentary on Henry Hammond's *Annotations on the New Testament* in 1683; it finally was published in 1698. And in 1699 there appeared *The Harmony of the Evangelists*. LeClerc's admiration for Hammond's work went back to the days when he had been in England and had used his texts to help him learn English. He placed Hammond "among the best Interpreters of the Holy Scriptures" and said that he knew "the difference between a Preacher or a Divine, and an Expositor of Scripture, [and that he set] himself to perform the part of an Interpreter, and seldom concern[ed] himself about any thing else."[49] To the translation, LeClerc added a supplement in which he supported Hammond's annotations and occasionally refuted them. The supplement was translated into English and LeClerc wrote a prefatory letter "to a Friend in *England*." This letter, directed primarily to the British, was a lively and informative presentation of his ideas on methodology in biblical criticism and of his appreciation of Hammond's work which had fallen into neglect and which deserved renewal of interest and appraisal of its excellent qualities.

He set down the rules by which a work ought to be judged; the requisites were overwhelming. The interpreter must know the language of the original; he must have full knowledge of the subject; he must acquire mastery of the author's style and method; he must have developed a critical habit, acquired in large measure by reading other interpreters. He said that although the general public could understand biblical criticism, there was real danger in popularizing works for which laymen were ill prepared.

The obstacles were formidable. LeClerc insisted that knowledge of English was insufficient "because the force of Arguments many times entirely depends upon knowing the use of the Greek Tongue, or Ecclesiastical or Profane History"; without this knowledge, safe judgments could not be made. Another obstacle was British hostility towards foreigners and foreign books. LeClerc wondered why the English, especially churchmen, were "displeased that the Books of Strangers should be read by their Countrymen"[50] and was baffled by the hostile reception accorded his own work by some of the clergy. He said that no man in Holland had bestowed more respect on the English clergy, and no one "speaks or writes oftner [*sic*] in their praise; and this not out of Flattery, . . . but because [he is] really of that mind."[51] He pointed out that he had done much to publicize British writings on the Continent so that "every one might have the benefit of the Learning of the English Nation" and hoped that this letter would help "remove the prejudices and misapprehensions of some People."[52]

LeClerc was so successful in reviving interest in Hammond's work that a "multitude of Copies" had been bought in all parts of Europe but his commentaries were attacked. In reply to those who said he had been overbold in correcting small errors, he argued that truth came before honor and that those who preferred perpetuation of error were "not fit to be spoken with."

He maintained that lapses in the works of great men were not immune to correction and should be modestly censured. Highest praise was not given to those who made the fewest mistakes but to those whose errors were few and insignificant. In his concluding remark he stated that truth must prevail, that it was greater than Hammond and that this work had not been published for Hammond's use "but [for] them who are now living, or for posterity, who may reasonably have a greater regard to Truth than to Dr. *Hammond*."[53]

From among the British attacks, LeClerc picked out for special attention the pamphlet entitled, *A Free but Modest Censure on the late Controversial Writings... Together with Brief Remarks on Monsieur LeClerc's 'Ars Critica'* by F. B., M. A. of Cambridge, printed in 1698, in which the writer saw in LeClerc's treatment of Hammond a plea for Socinianism. LeClerc took great pains to refute the critic who had asked, "When his Criticisms and Interpretations are blended with the Socinian ones, how easily will they be both imbibed together?" and who had warned the British to beware of "this hazard, that they may not be betrayed into Error... whilst they are intent upon studying the Truth."[54] LeClerc's defense rose well above the attack as he reiterated his general principle that truth would always prevail.[55] In a memorably personal passage, he declared, "I had infinitely rather stand in the number of the merciful, before the tribunal of the great Judg [sic], than in the company of Persecutors.... I had rather be ... evil spoken of and suspected of Errors... than appear by any means to countenance such Barbarity."[56]

His more particular defense against the charges of Socinianism was in allying himself with others who had also been falsely charged and viciously maligned. He cited as a notorious example that "worthy and ingenious Mr. *Lock* [sic], who, because he reasons more accurately about many things... in his Excellent Treatise of *Humane Understanding*, is immediately cried down as a *Socinian*."[57] He also recalled that Grotius and Descartes had been similarly attacked and that Erasmus had been charged with Arianism.

IX   The Harmony of the Evangelists

LeClerc said that he got the idea for *The Harmony of the Evangelists* after having read some pages on the subject in a projected book by Nicholas Toinard which he had received from the publisher, Daniel Elzevir. Finding Toinard obscure, he decided to write his own harmonium. It was translated into English in 1701. His main purpose was to justify variations in the Gospels. Through refinement of chronology of the years concerning the life of Christ and through better understanding of the writing of history, LeClerc ordered and selected material to help reduce if not to eradicate apparent differences among the writers of the Gospels. He observed that the historian was not obliged to account for every minute detail; instead, he should select material to achieve conciseness. Since historians worked independently, "'tis scarce possible that they should all hit upon the same circumstances throughout, or that a History should be abridg'd by every man in one method."⁵⁸

The translation found ready acceptance in England. Locke paid LeClerc a rare compliment when he wrote to Anthony Collins on January 24, 1703/4 asking for a copy "bound very finely in calf, gilt, and letter'd on the back, and guilt [sic] on the leaves."⁵⁹ In another letter, dated March 13, 1703/4, he told Collins that this copy was "for Mr. Secretary Johnston's Lady. The Book sent to his lodgings with a Note to inform him, that it is for his Lady from me, will do the business." And, on September 27, 1704, in a letter to Rev. Richard King, Locke, replying to a query as to the best way to understand the Scriptures, suggested reading either LeClerc's or Whiston's *Harmonia*. "They are now both in English, and Mr. LeClerc's has a Paraphrase. But if you read the Evangelists in the original, Mr. LeClerc's edition of his *Harmony* in Greek and Latin will be the best."⁶⁰

The translation had caused some commotion on the Continent and was eagerly anticipated in England. In a letter to Collins dated July 9, 1703, Locke wrote that he would like to see the French translation of LeClerc's Latin version. "I [had] expected one . . . from Holland ever since [it has] been out." And in another, dated October 1, 1703, he asked if LeClerc's *New Testament* was creating "any noise amongst the men of Letters or Divinity" in London. The reason for this query was that Locke had heard of the rough treatment it had received at the hands of the "Divines of Brandenburg or Cleve" who "have got the King of Prussia to prohibit it in his Dominions." Locke also told Collins that "the Walloon Divines in Holland are solliciting [*sic*] the same [prohibition] at the Hague." He admitted that these were only general reports and that he did not know the particular objections presented either by the Germans or by the Dutch, but he was disturbed because "If there be need of authentick Interpreters of the Word of God, what is the way to find them out?"[61]

Isaac Newton's correspondence with Locke contained a reference to LeClerc's biblical work. On December 13, 1691, Newton had written that "Dr Spencer ye Dean of Ely has perused ye specimen of LeClerck's [*sic*] latin [*sic*] version of ye Old Testament & likes ye designe [*sic*] very well but gives me no remarks upon it."[62] Spencer's approval was a fine endorsement when it is recalled that his *De Legibus Hebraeorum* has been credited with being the foundation of the science of comparative religion.

Despite Locke's sympathy, there was at least one instance where LeClerc found fault with him. Ever true to the principle of correcting errors, he said that he wished that Locke had not entered into an area outside the province of his greatest competence. In *Bibliothèque Choisie*, Tome XIII, he had dealt with Locke's explication of *Galatians*, iii, 20, and said that Locke would have done better had he been more "skilled in the critical knowledge of St. Paul's Expressions." He further stated that Locke had "read little in Divinity, that he often [made] Remarks upon things sufficiently known . . . that he often [passed] slightly over difficult places, or [said] nothing at all of them."

These comments were challenged by Robert Jenkins in *Remarks on . . . Lock's* [*sic*] *Paraphrases and Notes on St. Paul's Epistles . . .*, which was printed in London in 1709.[63] He said that these highly critical remarks arose from LeClerc's chagrin for having been omitted from the roster of authorities Locke had cited and that he was unwilling to accept LeClerc's "forc'd and far-fetched Interpretation." As a matter of fact, Jenkins said that he agreed with the remarks on Locke's low stature as a student of divinity.

This criticism of Locke was matched by comments on Isaac Newton. After LeClerc had read the two dissertations on Anti-Trinitarianism which he had agreed to translate, as was mentioned earlier, he told Locke that Newton would have improved his work had he "read with care what M. Simon has said on the subject, of which he speaks in his Criticism of the New Testament."

The works discussed in this chapter illustrate the cross-currents of ideas held in common by Dutch and British thinkers. LeClerc had been successful in bringing to Continental readers the best of British thinking and in generating vigorous discussion among the British themselves. His translated works were eagerly read, attacked and vilified; but the significant result was a renewal of awareness among the British of knotty problems posed when old ways were challenged.

CHAPTER 5

Conclusion

WITH the passage of more than two centuries, Jean LeClerc's work and influence have faded and dwindled until he is remembered, if at all, as a quarrelsome theologian whose impact upon his age was ephemeral and scarcely worth serious consideration. Yet, this study draws the inevitable conclusion that he was one of the foremost intermediaries in the movement of ideas between England and Holland during those germinal years from which the major intellectual forces of the eighteenth century drew so much of their strength and vitality.

Like Newton, Locke, Van Limborch, and others, he was convinced that the power of reason could remove obstacles which cluttered the way to truth and could eradicate myth, prejudice, superstition, and vanity. As an intermediary he explored, clarified, and disseminated the beliefs and the thoughts of those tough-minded British and Dutch thinkers who were reshaping their world by challenging hallowed traditions and unexamined conjectures which had dominated the past.

Through his *Bibliothèques* and his many other works, he labored to make the past intelligible, the present reasonable and, by combining both, to anticipate a prosperous future guided by the rational, the clear, and the cogent. The success of his work may be readily measured in the light of the intellectual milieu in England and on the Continent during the eighteenth century. His lifelong fight against sham, ignorance, and flattery ultimately prevailed and made a strong impact on thinkers who took up the cause of reason and enlightenment.

More specifically, LeClerc's writings touched on almost every important precinct in the republic of letters. His work in the field of classical scholarship led directly to better editions of the classics—editions distinguished by more accurate texts, more concise and informative notes, and more practical formats. He warned against the obstructive tactics of entrenched academicians

155

and against fragmentation of learning; he saw that the remedy
to combat decay of learning demanded an interdisciplinary outlook. In the area of literature LeClerc helped bring to the
general readership on the Continent the works of Addison,
Steele, Shaftesbury, Locke, and, to a lesser extent, Swift. Through
his *Bibliothèques* he compiled a useful record of perceptive,
critical commentary on these writers, praising their works as
moral forces.

One of his outstanding achievements was his role as publicist
in behalf of Locke's work at a time when it was little known
and little understood. Another was his dissemination of Newton's
ideas in the scientific communities in Holland and elsewhere.
Still another was his publication of excellent editions of Grotius
and Erasmus—these editions are still valuable.

His deep involvement in theological discussions and debates
resulted in his publicizing books and pamphlets and this brought
about the airing of ideas and information which otherwise
might have remained partially hidden and little noted. His
direct influence on British theological thinking has not yet been
fully assessed or appreciated. Through translation of British
writings into French and retranslation of summaries into English,
he made possible quick and easy access to ideas vital to British
divines. By exposure of opposing ideas, LeClerc played a major
role in upsetting long-held but unexamined points of view.

Historiography occupied much of his attention and he con-
sistently fought for the need of fresh appraisal of the past
through an orderly, scientific approach. He lifted the writing
of history out of the mire of myth and hearsay by insisting on
reliance on authenticated sources from which would come
reasonable conclusions and impartial interpretations. Objectivity
and honesty were his goals. By establishment of standards and
by codification of the intellectual equipment essential to the
good historian, he set sound principles.

Although LeClerc has never enjoyed the reputation of being
an original thinker, he merits such consideration for his efforts
to democratize learning and education. For him, humanity learning held no special mysteries and, consequently, he saw no need
for a priesthood of scholars, arguing that the intelligent layman
could be entrusted with what had been too long thought of as
the exclusive property of the self-appointed elite. In close
association with this belief, he held that there was urgent need

for better education of the young and that the responsibility rested on the shoulders of government. By such involvement he unwittingly prophesied public financial support of scholars.

In his devotion to expansion of knowledge among all who could benefit, he stripped away much of the veneer of exclusiveness threatening to stultify intellectual growth. His *Bibliothèques* served his cause. How right he was in his assessment of the need for expansion of learning may be noted by the widespread and enduring readership they enjoyed.

Examination of his works as they relate to the intellectual movements of his time reveal part of the strong foundation upon which rest the works of Locke, Newton, Shaftesbury, Van Limborch, Gruter, Burnet, and Bentley. The wide variety of enterprise, the interrelation of thoughts, the multifarious approaches to truth through reason, and the breaking of new ground to which the leading men of the day devoted their time are explained, discussed, debated, or cited in the works of LeClerc. Through him may be glimpsed the incredible complexity of the period.

Surely his work of expanding knowledge throughout the republic of letters clarified and simplified ideas which otherwise might have languished in obscurity. Its totality has earned him the right to be called the leading intermediary and the careful custodian of rationalism. Greater men have been treated fully, but as the period becomes better known and understood, Le-Clerc's role in it will call for renewed study of this man who was instrumental in promulgating the thought of the late seventeenth and early eighteenth centuries in England and in Holland.

Notes and References

Where applicable page references to quotations are incorporated into the text.

Abbreviations:
BUH   *Bibliothèque Universelle et Historique*
BC   *Bibliothèque Choisie*
BAM   *Bibliothèque Ancienne et Moderne*

Chapter One

1. "The Life of John Dryden," *The Miscellaneous Prose Works of Sir Walter Scott*, Robert Cadell (Edinburgh, 1841), I, 30.

2. John Tutchin, *The Foreigners* (London, 1700), p. 6. Also in John Tutchin, *Selected Poems*. The Augustan Reprint Society, Publication Number 110, 1964.

3. "An Explanatory Preface to the True-Born Englishman," *The Works of Daniel De Foe with a Memoir of his Life and Writings*, ed. William Hazlitt, J. Clements (London, 1843), III, 5.

4. *The Dutch Drawn to the Life . . .* (London, 1664), pp. 10, 48, 49, 58, 67.

5. *The Present State of the United Provinces of the Low-Countries; as to the Government, Laws, Forces, Riches, Manners, Customs, Revenues, and Territory, of the Dutch* (London, 1669), pp. 245, 339, 352, 353.

6. Bishop Burnet, *History of His Own Time*, William S. Orr (London, 1850), p. 883.

7. As quoted in J. A. Van der Welle, *Dryden and Holland* (Groningen: J. B. Wolters, 1962), pp. 96-97.

8. *Aanmerkingen Op Het Tractaat van Barriere en Het Tegen Project, Door den Schryver van Het Gedrag der Geallieerden* (Amsterdam: [Christiaan Petzold], 1712), Voorreden. It is included in *Tractaat Tusschen Hare Brittannische Majesteit en de Hoog Mog. Heeren Staten General . . .* (Amsterdam, 1712), p. 118. This quotation may well be the first notice of Swift on the continent even though the writer was unaware that Swift had written *The Conduct of the Allies*.

9. David C. Douglas, *English Scholars 1660-1730* (London: Eyre & Spottiswoode, 1951), *passim*.

10. Sir Thomas Browne, *Hydriotaphia*, as quoted in Douglas, *English Scholars 1660-1730*, p. 29.

159

11. John Dryden, *Of Dramatic Poesy and Other Critical Essays,* ed. George Watson (London: J. M. Dent, 1962), II, 164.

12. Alexander Pope, *The Dunciad,* in Twickenham Edition, ed. James Sutherland (London: Methuen, 1963), V, 123n.

13. *Ibid.,* Book IV, 11. 149-60.

14. W. J. B. Pienaar, *English Influences in Dutch Literature* (Cambridge: Cambridge University Press, 1929), p. 28.

15. Among these were the following with dates of election: Henry Justel (Dec. 7, 1681); Gregory Leti (Nov. 30, 1681); Jacques de Beauval (Nov. 30, 1697); Peter Des Maizeaux (Nov. 30, 1720).

16. H. John McLachlan, *Socinianism in Seventeenth-Century England* (London: Oxford University Press, 1951), p. 30.

17. Aharon Lichtenstein, *Henry More—The Rational Theology of a Cambridge Platonist* (Cambridge: Harvard University Press, 1962), p. 123.

18. Van der Welle, p. 83.

19. Theodor Weevers, *Poetry of the Netherlands in its European Context 1170-1930* (London: The Athlone Press, 1960), p. 146.

20. See my articles, "Benjamin Furly's Library: An Intermediary Source in Anglo-Dutch Literary Relations," *Hermathena,* No. XCVI, 1962, pp. 16-20. *"Bibliotheca Furliana* Revisited," *The Journal of the Friends' Historical Society,* Vol. 50, No. 2, 1962, 72-76.

21. Guy H. Dodge, *The Political Theory of the Huguenots of the Dispersion with Special Reference to the Thought and Influence of Pierre Jurieu* (New York: Columbia University Press, 1947), p. 41.

22. Pienaar, p. 2.

23. James William Johnson, *The Formation of English Neo-Classical Thought* (Princeton, N. J.: Princeton University Press, 1967), p. 164.

24. Van der Welle, p. 10.

25. Annie Barnes, *Jean LeClerc (1657-1736) et la République Des Lettres* (Paris: Libraire E. Droz, 1938), p. 135.

26. Betty T. Morgan, *Histoire du Journal des Sçavans depuis 1665 Jusqu'en 1701* (Paris: Les Presses Universitaires de France, 1929), p. 195.

27. Hilda J. Reesink, *L'Angleterre et la Littérature Anglaise dans les Trois plus Anciens Périodiques Français de Hollande de 1684 à 1709* (Paris: Libraire Champion, 1931), p. 22.

28. Leslie Stephen, *History of English Thought in the Eighteenth Century* (New York: Harcourt, Brace & World, 1962), II, 16.

29. Paul Hazard, *European Thought in the Eighteenth Century,* tr. J. Lewis May (New York: World Publishing Co., 1963), p. 37.

30. Rosalie L. Colie, *Light and Enlightenment* (Cambridge: Cambridge University Press, 1957), p. 31 and Chapter VII, *passim.*

31. John J. Murray, *Amsterdam in the Age of Rembrandt* (Nor-

man, Oklahoma: University of Oklahoma Press, 1967), p. 91.

32. Barnes, p. 96.

Chapter Two

1. Van der Welle, p. 112.

2. The biographical details and the source of pertinent quotations are from *An Account of the Life and Writings of Mr. John Le Clerc* (London, 1712). This work is autobiographical. Page numbers of quotations from this book are in the text.

3. Leti was an outspoken historian and a leader in the movement to treat events and persons without regard for traditional flattery.

4. The Fourth Dialogue is worth recalling. In it, LeClerc said later that he was anticipating John Locke's notions of "Properties" as were to be explained four years later in *An Essay Concerning Human Understanding*. LeClerc had argued that we should limit our sense to those things which we can comprehend and if we exceed their limits we fall into error. ". . . as we received not our Senses, with a Design to pry into the internal Nature of things, which is hidden from them, but that we should use them for the Preservation of Life. . . . If we once begin to exceed these Bounds, we voluntarily throw our selves into unavoidable Danger of Error." With pardonable pride, LeClerc reported that in Locke's famous essay he found himself "afterwards very much confirm'd in this Opinion."

5. LeClerc seldom mentioned his private life. Among the few personal remarks is the following: "he married Mary Leti, the Daughter of Gregory Leti, by whom he had Four Children, but all of them dy'd in their Infancy. One of them, nam'd Gregory, a Boy of a fine Wit and Complexion, liv'd to the 8th Year of his Age, in which, being consum'd by a long Disease, he dy'd, to the Eternal Grief of his sorrowful Parents" (p. 65).

6. MS., Universiteits Bibliotheek, Amsterdam, 76b. Annie Barnes has noted this letter and has suggested that Burnet did not want LeClerc in England because of the differences in their characters. *Op. cit.*, p. 161.

7. Maurice Cranston, *John Locke* (London: Longmans, Green, 1957), p. 416n. D'Aranda overstated the case. According to Cranston, d'Aranda had written to Locke that LeClerc had a wife and six children, was without an income, and was unable to get charity.

8. *Some Familiar Letters Between Mr. Locke, and Several of his Friends,* [no ed.] (London, 1708), p. 170.

9. *Ibid.*, pp. 178-79.

10. *Ibid.*, p. 186.

11. *Loc. cit.*

12. *Ibid.*, p. 187.

13. *Ibid.*, p. 231.

14. *Ibid.*, p. 235.

15. MS., Universiteits Bibliotheek, Amsterdam, J1.

16. For Wasse's complete letter, see Amorie van der Hoeven, *De Joanne Clerico et Philippo a Limborch* (Amsterdam: F. Muller, 1843), p. 279.

17. *An Account of the Life and Writings*, p. 64.

18. Lynn Thorndike, *A History of Magic and Experimental Science* (New York: Columbia University Press, 1958), VIII, 617.

19. McKenzie, I, 100, 166. See Appendix L. LeClerc's *Physica* and other texts were not so readily acceptable at Oxford. James Tyrrell had written to Locke (February 28, 1703) that one of the heads of colleges (probably Dr. Mill of St. Edmund Hall) had recommended that "the tutors . . . should be advised neither to read your [Locke's] *Essay* [*i.e. Essay Concerning Human Understanding*] nor Le Clerc's *Physica* nor *Logica* to their pupils, since those works had much discouraged the noble art of disputation." As quoted in Cranston, p. 467.

20. James Luther Adams, "Arminius and the Structure of Society," in *Man's Faith and Freedom: The Theological Influence of Jacobus Arminius*, ed. Gerald O. McCulloch (New York: Abingdon Press, 1962), pp. 88-89.

21. The title page reads as follows: "Portion of an unfinished Translation of LeClerc's 'Ars Critica.'" Vol. I. By The Rev. Charles Andrews Farley. Cambridge. Printed at the University Press, 183-. Penciled in on this page of the copy at Harvard College is the notation, "April 7, 1853 Gift of Charles Folsom." But the work was originally presented as a gift to the Boston Athenaeum, as indicated on page 1 and was acquired by Harvard College on Nov. 22, 1904, as shown by a rubber-stamped inscription on the same page. It ends abruptly. This printed portion has the handwritten notation, "No more was printed," which seems to indicate that Farley had translated more but that further printing had been abandoned. Attempts to locate the whole MS have been fruitless. Neither the Boston Athenaeum nor Harvard College has it, nor knows, if it is still extant.

22. BC Tome VII, Article X.

23. *An Account of the Life and Writings*, Letter VI, p. 72.

24. MS., Universiteits Bibliotheek, Amsterdam, 17a.

25. *Ibid.*, J17c and J54. The Archbishop's account was followed by a letter to Chamberlayne on June 8, 1708.

> Monsieur
>> Ce fut avec bien de regret que je me trouvois contraint de rendre une telle conte de Monsieur de Gabillon, qui sera si au grè aux enemis de la verité. Neanmoins cela me consoler, que pas a

moyens je vous ay rendu justice car je suis avec
beacoup de respect.

Monsieur,
Votre
Archbishop of London

26. *Ibid.*, C112.
27. *Ibid.*, J17d.
28. *Loc. cit.*
29. *Ibid.*, J17e.
30. *An Account of the Life and Writings*, p. 57.
31. *A Funeral Oration upon the Death of M. Philip Limborch...* (London, 1713).
32. *An Oration Concerning the Excellence and Usefulness of Ecclesiastical History* (London, [n.d.]), p. 15.
33. See Wasse's letter in Hoeven, p. 279.
34. R. C. Jebb, *Bentley (English Men of Letters Series)* (New York: Harper & Brothers, [n.d.]), p. 122.
35. *Mr. LeClerc's Judgment and Censure of Dr. Bentley's Horace; and of the Amsterdam Edition, Compar'd with that of Cambridge.* (London, 1713), p. 10.
36. *Ibid.*, p. 8.
37. BC Tome XIX, Article XI.
38. It was printed at Utrecht, "chez Guillaume vander Water, Imprimeur de l'Academie."

Chapter Three

1. The dates in parentheses indicate date of beginning of auction.
2. See Reesink, pp. 399-406, for a list of British works translated into Dutch before 1710.
3. Watson, II, 240.
4. Cranston's assertion that Locke "wrote nearly everything which was published there between *July 1687* and *February 1688*" is based on his acceptance of Laslett's study of the marginalia of Locke's own copy of BUH and his conclusion that Locke had written for Volumes VI-VIII: VI, 1-127, 229-236, 277-311; VII, 1-49, 85-320; VIII, 1-261. Cranston, p. 293 and 293n.
5. *Parrhasiana*, Pt. I, p. 272.
6. *The Life and Character of Mr. John Locke*, tr., T. F. P. (London, 1706), p. 4.
7. *Ibid.*, p. 15.
8. Reesink, p. 237. See also Cranston for Proast's remarks on Locke's work, p. 331 ff.
9. In May, 1691, the French translation of *Two Treatises of Government* was mentioned in a brief announcement of only two-and-a-half pages. David Mazel's translation was praised by LeClerc,

especially for the excellence of its preface defending Locke's arguments against those who based their ideas not on general principles but on their experiences in their own countries, especially in France.

10. As quoted in Kenneth Dewhurst, *Dr. Thomas Sydenham (1624-1689) His Life and Original Writings* (Berkeley: University of California Press, 1966), p. 56. A personal connection between LeClerc and Sydenham is related in Dewhurst's *John Locke (1632-1704) Physician and Philosopher* (London: The Wellcome Historical Medical Library, 1963), pp. 233-34. "At the beginning of 1688 LeClerc was ill, and Locke referred his case to Drs. Sydenham and Goodall, who recommended some pills, an elixir of gentium, and a course of German spa waters."

11. Thomas Baker, *Reflections upon Learning* (London, 1700), p. 86.

12. Thorndike, VII, 615.

13. Bayle and Basnage also reported on this dispute. For Bayle, see *Nouvelles,* Nov., 1685, Oct., 1686. For Basnage, see *Ouvrages des Sçavans,* Nov., 1687.

14. For a complete list of Burnet's works mentioned in BUH, see Reesink, pp. 208-11.

15. LeClerc, *The Life of Dr. Burnet . . . and an Account of his Writings,* tr. into *English* from his last *Bibliothèque* (London, 1715), p. 4.

16. Reesink, pp. 214-15, lists eight works by Clagett.

17. LeClerc, *A Defence of Archbishop Tillotson, and his Writings* (London, 1696), p. 2:

18. LeClerc, *The Harmony of the Evangelists* (London, 1701), p. 616.

19. See Reesink, pp. 233, 236.

20. MS., Universiteits Bibliotheek, Amsterdam, J60a, J60b and J60c, dated respectively May 4, 1710, July 9, 1710, and November 9, 1710, deal with Theophrastus.

21. The issues, not necessarily complicated, are blurred by their unfortunate nomenclature. Hylozoick followers believed that matter was endowed with life; plastic nature was a belief in "a creative spiritual force inherent in the universe and in its substantial parts." Colie, p. 123. J. A. Passmore, *Ralph Cudworth* (Cambridge: Cambridge University Press, 1951), pp. 1-28.

22. Evidence "is the mark of truth, which, when present, makes impossible to doubt a proposition." Richard H. Popkin, *Selections from Pierre Bayle's Historical and Critical Dictionary* (New York: The Bobbs-Merrill Co., 1965), p. 199n. Quoting from Furetière's *Dictionnaire Universelle* (1727), Popkin cites the following as LeClerc's view on *l'évidence*: "The criterion of truth is *l'évidence*, which cannot be resisted as soon as it makes itself felt in us. . . .

Notes and References

165

L'évidence is the essential and infallible mark of truth, and if an *evidently* true proposition were ultimately false, then God himself would be the cause of our error."

23. Colie, p. 139.

24. *An Account of the Life and Writings,* p. 45.

25. Colie, p. 142.

26. *Loc. cit.*

27. *Loc. cit.*

28. "Mr. LeClerc's Extract and Judgment of *The Rights of the Christian Church asserted* &c." Translated from his *Bibliothèque Choisie,* Tome X. To which is prefix'd, A Letter to a Noble Peer . . . (London, 1708).

29. *Ibid.,* p. 2.

30. Of digressive interest is Hickes's remarks on John Dryden. The passage is worth quoting not only to show in what low esteem the poet was held at this time but also to show how, among some of the clergy, the opposite positions of Dryden, a Catholic, and of LeClerc, an Arminian, were the object of the same kind of attack. Hickes wrote of Dryden in the preface as follows: "The Apostate Poet, who did us the honour to forsake our Church; that great corrupter of the Stage, and Age, whose *Apollo* was *Apollyon* and *Blasphemy* his *Muse*; that *Chairman* in the Meetings of the Scorners, who is gone to give an account of his Works, was the first Writer, who took upon him, after the Restauration [*sic*], to bring all the Disgrace his Muse or Malice could invent upon the Clergy; and at last to tell the World, that Priests of all Religions were the same."

31. *A Letter to the Reverend Dr. Moss in Behalf of The Rights of the Christian Church. Together with a Poetick Rhapsody. By a Young Oxford-Scholar.* Printed for B. Bragg in Paternoster-Row, 1709. The writer refers to Tindal as the author of *The Rights* without question.

32. Samuel Hilliard, *A Narrative of the Prosecution of Mr. Sare* . . . (London, 1709), p. 16.

33. BC Tome XVIII.

34. David Brewster, *Memoirs of the Life, Writings, and Discoveries of Sir Isaac Newton* (Edinburgh: Thomas Constable and Co., 1855), II, 326.

35. Alexandre Koyré, *Newtonian Studies* (London: Chapman and Hall, 1965), p. 5.

36. MS., Universiteits Bibliotheek, Amsterdam, J3a, J3b.

37. Shaftesbury, "Miscellaneous Reflections," in *Characteristics,* ed. John M. Robertson (New York: The Bobbs-Merrill Co., 1964), p. 167. See BC Tome XIX.

38. *Ibid.,* p. 168.

39. *Ibid.,* p. 289.

40. *Ibid.*, p. 305.

41. It was translated by Lewis Theobald, long an admirer of Addison. In 1713 Theobald had written a life of Cato as supplementary reading for Addison's *Cato*. In the dedication addressed to Eustace Budgell, he lavishly praised Addison. "All the Writings of Mr. Addison have something in 'em so above the Pitch of modern Compositions, that they are as easy to be Distinguish'd from others, as they are impossible to be Imitated."

42. The long title is self-explanatory: *Acta Regia: or, An Account of the Treaties, Letters and Instruments Between the Monarchs of England and Foreign Powers, publish'd in Mr. Rymer's FOEDERA,* . . . Translated from the French of Mr. Rapin, as publish'd by M. LeClerc. With the Heads of the Kings and Queens, curiously engrav'd by Mr. Vandergucht. To be Publish'd Monthly. . . . The translator was also the writer of the dedication to William Benson.

43. Calhoun Winton, *Captain Steele* (Baltimore: The Johns Hopkins Press, 1964), pp. 74 and 152.

44. In *Nouvelles de la République,* March and April, 1717, edited by LeClerc, Pope's work was mentioned among new books available in Amsterdam.

Chapter Four

1. *Parrhasiana: or, Thoughts upon Several Subjects; as, Criticism, History, Morality, and Politics.* By Monsieur *Le Clerk,* under the feigned Name of *Theodorus Parrhasi.* Done into *English* by °°°°, (London, 1700).

2. *An Account of the Life and Writings,* p. 33.

3. *Parrhasiana,* pp. 161 and 162.

4. *Parrhasiana ou Pensées Diverses Sur des Matières De Critique, D'Histoire, De Morale et De Politique.* Par Theodore Parrhase. Tome Second. A Amsterdam, Chez Henri Schelte, 1701.

5. *Parrhasiana,* p. 259.

6. *Ibid.*, pp. 259-60.

7. In Letter V, LeClerc quoted from a recent Dutch translation of Richard Baxter's *The Saints' Everlasting Rest.*

8. C. G. Lamothe, *The Inspiration of the New Testament asserted and explained, in answer to some modern Writers* (London, 1694).

9. W. Lowth, *A Vindication of the Divine Authority and Inspiration of the Old and New Testament.* In Answer to a Treatise Lately Translated out of the French, Entitled, *Five Letters concerning the Inspiration of the Holy Scriptures,*—The second edition,—Printed by William Horton, for John Wilmot Bookseller in Oxford (London, 1699), preface. The first edition came out in 1692.

10. This edition is a reprinting of the second. LeClerc's work, too, lasted well into the eighteenth century. There appeared in 1750

Free and Important Disquisitions Concerning Inspiration of the Holy Scriptures ... Translated *from the Original French of the Celebrated M. Le Clerc.*

This edition follows almost exactly the original English translation until the end of the first Letter. The second Letter omits the first part of its original counterpart; both Letters are fused into one and the remaining ones are omitted.

11. *An Account of the Life and Writings,* p. 30.
12. *Parrhasiana,* pp. 286-87.
13. *Ibid.,* pp. 287-88.
14. *Ibid.,* p. 289.
15. BUH Tomes VIII, X, XII, and XVIII.
16. LeClerc, *The Lives of the Primitive Fathers* (London, 1701), p. 39.
17. *Ibid.,* p. 188.
18. *Ibid.,* p. 39.
19. *Parrhasiana,* p. 288.
20. *An Account of the Life and Writings,* p. 33.
21. LeClerc, *Reflections upon what the World Commonly Call Good-Luck and Ill-Luck, with Regard to Lotteries. And of the Good Use which may be made of them.* Written Originally in French. . . . Done into English. Printed for Matth. Gillyflower in Westminster-Hall, Tim. Goodwin, Matth. Wotton, and B. Tooke in Fleetstreet, 1699.
22. *Ibid.,* p. 4.
23. *Ibid.,* p. 1.
24. *Ibid.,* p. 67.
25. *Loc. cit.*
26. *Ibid.,* p. 159.
27. *Ibid.,* p. 162.
28. *Parrhasiana,* p. 247.
29. *Ibid.,* p. 248.
30. The British Museum catalog lists editions in 1718, 1724, 1734, 1745, 1755, 1817, 1821, 1836. See BC Tome XVIII.
31. *An Account of the Life and Writings,* p. 58.
32. *Ibid.,* p. 59.
33. *Ibid.,* p. 60.
34. *Ibid.,* p. 50.
35. *Ibid.,* pp. 52-53.
36. BC Tomes V and VI.
37. *An Account of the Life and Writings,* p. 56.
38. *Ibid.,* p. 53.
39. *Ibid.,* p. 54.
40. John Jortin, *The Life of Erasmus* (London, 1758), preface.
41. Baker, p. 188.

42. Robert Masters, *Memoirs of the Life and Writings of the Late Rev. Thomas Baker . . . From the papers of Dr. Zachary Grey* (Cambridge, 1784), p. 17. See LeClerc's *Ars Critica*, 4th ed. under "Erasmus."

43. *An Account of the Life and Writings*, pp. 56-57.

44. *Ibid.*, p. 58.

45. MS., Koninklijke Bibliotheek, The Hague, 130G30.

46. *Parrhasiana*, p. 282.

47. BC Tome IV, Article X.

48. LeClerc, *Additions to Dr. Hammond's Annotations on the New Testament* (London, 1699), p. xxiii.

49. LeClerc, *A Supplement to Dr. Hammond's Paraphrase and Annotations on the New Testament* (London, 1699), p. vii.

50. *Ibid.*, p. iii.

51. *Ibid.*, p. iv.

52. *Loc. cit.*

53. *Ibid.*, p. ix.

54. *Ibid.*, p. x.

55. *Loc. cit.*

56. *Ibid.*, p. xi.

57. *Ibid.*, p. xii.

58. *The Harmony of the Evangelists*, p. 588.

59. *A Collection of Several Pieces of Mr. John Locke . . .* (London, 1720), p. 295.

60. *Ibid.*, p. 355.

61. *Ibid.*, p. 264.

62. *The Correspondence of Isaac Newton*, ed. H. W. Turnbull (Cambridge: Cambridge University Press, 1961), III, 185-86.

63. The British Museum copy attributes the work to "Dr. Robt. Jenkin." On the fly leaf, in pencil, "By Dr. Jenkin's [*sic*] Chaplain to Lord Weymouth and the learned Margaret Prof. of the University of Cambridge & Master of St. John's Coll."

Selected Bibliography

There is no complete bibliography of LeClerc's works. The most comprehensive one is in MM. Eug. et Em. Haag, *La France Protestante ou Vies des Protestante Français,* 9 Vols. (Geneva: Joel Cherbuliez, 1846), VI, 465-70. This listing numbers seventy-three works with brief annotations for thirty. LeClerc's *An Account of the Life and Writings* lists works written up to 1711. Brief listings occur in standard English, Dutch, and French encyclopedias. In general, primary source material is severely limited to works translated into English.

PRIMARY SOURCES

LeClerc, Jean. *Bibliothèque Universelle et Historique,* 1686-1693, 26 Vols. Wolfgang, Waesberge, Boom, and van Someren. Amsterdam.

————. *Bibliothèque Choisie,* pour Servir de suite à la *Bibliothèque Universelle,* 1703-1713, 28 Vols. H. Schelte. Amsterdam.

————. *Bibliothèque Ancienne et Moderne,* pour Servir de suite aux *Bibliothèques Universelle et Choisie,* 1714-1727, 29 Vols. D. Mortier, 1714-19; Les Frères Wetstein, 1719-26: Amsterdam. P. Husson, 1727-30: The Hague.

Bayle, Pierre, Jacques Bernard and others. *Nouvelles de la République des Lettres,* 1684-1689, 15 Vols. Henri Desbordes. Amsterdam.

Basnage de Beauval, Henri. *Histoires des Ouvrages des Sçavans,* 1687-1709, 24 Vols. R. Leers. Rotterdam.

Rabus, Pierre. *Boekzaal van Europa,* 1692-1705, 9 Vols. P. van der Slaart. Rotterdam.

Sewel, Willem. *Boekzaal der Geleerde Wereld,* 1705-1706, 4 Vols. P. van der Slaart. Rotterdam.

MS., Bibliothèque de l'Eglise des Remonstrants, Rotterdam.
LeClerc-Bentley Correspondence, 1710.

MS., Koninklijke Bibliotheek, The Hague.
LeClerc-Cuper Correspondence. 72G17.
LeClerc-Burnet Correspondence. 130G30.

MS., Lambeth Palace Library, London.
LeClerc-Nicholls Correspondence. No. 3 and 16.

MS., Universiteits Bibliotheek, Amsterdam.
*LeClerc-Bentley Correspondence. K14a-b.

LeClerc-Berkeley Correspondence. J3a-b.
LeClerc-Burnet Correspondence. J76a-f.
LeClerc-Chamberlayne Correspondence. J17a-e.
LeClerc-Fletcher Correspondence. J29.
LeClerc-Gagnier Correspondence. J32.
LeClerc-Kidder Correspondence. J49.
LeClerc-Lady Masham Correspondence. J82b.
LeClerc-Milbourne Correspondence. C93.
LeClerc-Needham Correspondence. J60a-c.
LeClerc-Saurin Correspondence. C124.
LeClerc-Wotton Correspondence. K90a-e.
De la Loge-Desmoiseaux Correspondence. C112.
*See Epistolarum J. Clerici in *Epistolae ad Anglois*, III, D24.

LeClerc, Jean. *Sentimens de Quelques Théologiens de Hollande sur l'Histoire Critique du Vieux Testament*, Composée par le P. Richard Simon de l'Oratoire. (Amsterdam: H. Desbordes, 1685).

———. *Five Letters Concerning the Inspiration of the Holy Scriptures*. (London, 1690).

———. *A Defence of Archbishop Tillotson and his Writings*. (London, 1696).

———. *Twelve Dissertations out of LeClerk's Genesis*, tr. Mr. Brown. (London, 1696).

———. *A Treatise of the Causes of Incredulity*, tr. Mr. Sault. (London, 1697).

———. *Additions to Dr. Hammond's Annotations on the New Testament*. (London, 1699).

———. *A Compendium of Universal History*. (London, 1699).

———. *Reflections upon what the World Commonly Call Good-Luck and Ill-Luck, with Regard to Lotteries. And of the Good Use which may be made of them*. (London, 1699).

———. *A Supplement to Dr. Hammond's Paraphrase and Annotations on the New Testament*. (London, 1699).

———. *Parrhasiana: or, Thoughts upon Several Subjects; as, Criticism, History, Morality, and Politics*. By Monsieur Le Clerk, under the feigned Name of *Theodorus Parrhasi*. Done into *English* by ****. (London, 1700).

———. *The Harmony of the Evangelists, being The Whole Text of the Four Gospels dispos'd according to the Order of Time in which the Things related in them were done*.... (London, 1701).

———. *The Lives of the Primitive Fathers, viz. Clemens Alexandrinus, Eusebius, Bishop of Caesarea, Gregory Nazianzen, and Prudentius the Christian Poet*. (London, 1701).

———. *Parrhasiana ou Pensées Diverses Sur des Matières De*

Critique, D'Histoire, De Morale et De Politique. Par Theodore Parrhase. Tome Second. A Amsterdam, Chez Henri Schelte, 1701.

————. *The Life and Character of Mr. John Locke, Author of the Essay concerning Humane Understanding* . . . And done into English, by T. F. P. Gent. (London, 1706).

————. *Extract and Judgment of The Rights of the Christian Church asserted, &c.* Translated from his *Bibliothèque Choisie,* Tome X. To which is prefix'd, A Letter to a Noble Peer. . . . (London, 1708).

————. *Account of the Earl of Clarendon's History of the Civil Wars,* tr. J[ohn] O[zell]. (London, 1710).

————. *The Rights of the Christian Church Adjusted: Being the Extract and Judgment of Mr. LE CLERC upon those AUTHORS who have Written against [The Book Intitul'd] The Rights of the Christian Church Asserted &c, viz. Dr. HICKES, Dr. TURNER, Mr. WOTTON, Mr. HILL, Mr. CAROL, Mr. OLDS-WORTH &c.* (London, 1711).

————. *An Account of the Life and Writings* . . . To this present Year M DCC XI. To which is added, A Collection of Letters, from J. G. GRAEVIUS, and Baron SPANHEIM, to Mr. LE CLERC. (London, 1712).

————. *Extract and Judgment of the Characteristicks of Men, Manners, Opinions, Times* [by the Earl of Shaftesbury]. (London, 1712).

————. *An Abstract and Judgment of D^r. Clark's (Rector of St. James's) Polemical or Controversial Writings.* (London, 1713).

————. *A Funeral Oration upon the Death of Philip Limborch.* (London, 1713).

————. *Judgment and Censure of Dr. Bentley's Horace; and of the Amsterdam Edition, Compar'd with that of Cambridge.* (London, 1713).

————. *The Life of Dr. Burnet, Late Lord Bishop of Sarum; with his Character, and an Account of his Writings.* Translated into English, from his last *Bibliothèque.* (London, 1715).

————. *Observations upon Mr. Addison's Travels through Italy,* &c., tr. Mr. Theobald. (London, 1715).

————. *The Truth of the Christian Religion* . . . To which is added, "What Christian Church we ought to Join our Selves to," tr. John Clarke. (London, 1719).

————. *A Critical Examination of the Reverend Mr. Dean Prideaux's Connection of the Old and New Testament.* (London, 1722).

————. "Criticism upon Quintus Curtius" in Arrianus, *History of Alexander's Expedition,* tr. J. Rooke. 2 Vols. (London, 1729).

————. "On Inspiration" and John Locke, "Essay for the Understanding of St. Paul's Epistles," ed. Andrews Norton (Boston: Wells and Lilly, 1820).

SECONDARY SOURCES

Writings in the late seventeenth and eighteenth centuries:

ANON. *An Answer to Mr. de Fontenelle's History of Oracles . . . with Some Reflections upon the Remarks of Mr. Le Clerc, in his Bibliothèque Choisie. . . .* By a Priest of the Church of England. To which is prefix'd a Letter to the translator, by the Reverend George Hickes. (London, 1709).

————. *A Letter to the Reverend Dr. Moss in Behalf of The Rights of the Christian Church. Together with a Poetick Rhapsody. By a Young Oxford-Scholar.* Printed for B. Bragg in Paternoster-Row, 1709.

B., F., *A Free but Modest Censure on the late Controversial Writings and Debates. . . . Together with Brief Remarks on Monsieur Le Clerc's Ars Critica.* [no place of publication, 1698].

BAKER, THOMAS. *Reflections upon Learning.* The second edition. (London, 1700).

BURMAN, PIETER. *Le Gazettier Menteur, ou Mr. LeClerc Convaincu de Mensonge & Calomnie.* (Utrecht, 1710).

HILLIARD, SAMUEL. *A Narrative of the Prosecution of Mr. Sare and his Servant, for Selling the Rights of the Christian Church.* (London, 1709).

JENKIN, ROBERT. *Remarks on some Books Lately Publish'd,* viz. Basnage's History of the *Jews,* Whiston's Eight Sermons, Lock's [*sic*] Paraphrase and Notes on St. *Paul's* Epistles, LeClerc's Bibliothèque Choisie. (London, 1709).

JORTIN, JOHN. *The Life of Erasmus.* 2 Vols. (London, 1758).

KENNET, DR. [?]. *Reflections upon some Passages in Mr. LeClerc's Life of M^r. John Locke*: in a Letter to a Friend. (London, 1711).

LAMOTHE, C. G. *The Inspiration of the New Testament asserted and explained, in answer to some modern Writers.* (London, 1694).

[LOCKE, JOHN]. *A Collection of Several Pieces of Mr. John Locke, Never before printed, or not extant in any of his Works,* ed. DesMaizeaux [?]. (London, 1720).

————. *Some Familiar Letters between Mr. Locke, and Several of his Friends.* (London, 1708).

LOWTH, WILLIAM. *A Vindication of the Divine Authority and Inspiration of the Old and New Testament.* In Answer to a Treatise Lately Translated out of the *French,* Entitled, *Five Letters concerning the Inspiration of the Holy Scriptures,*—The second edition,—Printed by William Horton, for John Wilmot Bookseller in Oxford. (London, 1699).

MASTERS, ROBERT. *Memoirs of the Life and Writings of the Late Rev. Thomas Baker* . . . From the papers of Dr. Zachary Grey. (Cambridge, 1784).

[SIMON, RICHARD]. *Réponse au Livre intitulé: Sentimens de Quelques Théologiens de Hollande sur l'Histoire Critique du Vieux Testament.* Par le Prieur de Bolleville [pseud.] R. Leers (Rotterdam, 1686).

Modern commentary and background material:

BACHRACH, A. G. H. *Sir Constantine Huygens and Britain: 1596-1687,* Vol. I (1596-1619). (London: Oxford University Press, 1962). One of the best scholarly studies in describing an important Anglo-Dutch relationship.

BARNES, ANNIE. *Jean LeClerc (1657-1736) et la République Des Lettres.* (Paris: E. Droz, 1938). A steady recital of facts.

BAYLE, PIERRE. *Historical and Critical Dictionary,* tr. Richard H. Popkin. (New York: The Bobbs-Merrill Company, Inc., 1965).

BREWSTER, SIR DAVID. *Memoirs of the Life, Writings, and Discoveries of Sir Isaac Newton.* 2 Vols. (Edinburgh: Thomas Constable and Co., 1855). A good biography to illuminate and to clarify Newton's role in the movement of the new science.

COLIE, ROSALIE L. *Light and Enlightenment* (Cambridge: Cambridge University Press, 1957). This slender volume has become a minor masterpiece in its attempt to unravel Anglo-Dutch religious problems. The section on Cudworth and LeClerc is essential.

————. *'Some Thankfulnesse to Constantine': A Study of English Influence upon the Early Works of Constantijn Huygens* (The Hague: Martinus Nijhoff, 1956). This is a good book to be read in conjunction with Bachrach's.

CRANSTON, MAURICE. *John Locke* (London: Longmans, Green and Co., 1957). A scholarly, well documented biography in which LeClerc's relationship with Locke is given its proper place.

DEBUS, ALLEN G., AND ROBERT P. MULTHAUF. *Alchemy and Chemistry in the Seventeenth Century* (Los Angeles: William A. Clark Memorial Library, 1966). Affords a quick view of scientific thought. A monograph.

DEWHURST, KENNETH. *John Locke (1632-1704) Physician and Philosopher* (London: The Wellcome Historical Medical Library, 1963). A lively account, especially useful for its study of Anglo-Dutch scientific relations.

————. *Dr. Thomas Sydenham (1624-1689) His Life and Original Writings* (Berkeley: University of California Press, 1966). A systematic account of his achievements in medicine with concentration on Sydenham's reputation among the Dutch.

DODGE, GUY H. *The Political Theory of the Huguenots of the Dispersion with Special Reference to the Thought and Pierre Jurieu* (New York: Columbia University Press, 1947). A necessary book for an understanding of Pierre Jurieu in particular and of his place among the Dutch refugees from France.

DOUGLAS, DAVID C. *English Scholars 1660-1730* (London, Eyre & Spottiswoode, 1951). An invaluable compilation of studies of scholars who were influential in fostering British learning. Chapter X, "Clerics in Controversy," is very helpful.

FORSTER, LEONARD. *Janus Gruter's English Years* (London, Oxford University Press, 1967). A brief but complete study of Dutch poetry in the sixteenth century. Of special interest is treatment of life of Dutch exiles in Elizabethan England.

HARRISON, JOHN, AND PETER LASLETT. *The Library of John Locke* (Oxford: Oxford University Press, 1965). A catalogue worth examining, especially for its listing of LeClerc's works.

HAZARD, PAUL. *European Thought in the Eighteenth Century* (New York: The World Publishing Company, 1963). One of the most popular and exciting books on a vast scale.

HOEVEN, AMORIE VAN DER. *De Joanne Clerico et Philippo a Limborch* (Amsterdam: F. Muller, 1843). A disjointed text, but valuable for its facts and its printing of contemporary correspondence. Has never been translated from the Latin.

JEBB, R. C. *Bentley* (New York: Harper & Brothers, 1882). Somewhat dated, but still a straightforward biography packed with pertinent details.

JOHNSON, JAMES WILLIAM. *The Formation of English Neo-Classical Thought* (Princeton: Princeton University Press, 1967). The best modern study of the subject. Chapter VII is excellent for its treatment of Holland.

KOYRÉ, ALEXANDRE. *Newtonian Studies* (London: Chapman and Hall, 1965). A serious, mature work excellent as background reading.

[LOCKE, JOHN]. *Lettres inédites de John Locke*, eds. M. Henry Ollion and T. J. de Boer. (The Hague: Martinus Nijhoff, 1912).

MANUEL, FRANK E. *The Eighteenth Century Confronts the Gods* (Cambridge: Harvard University Press, 1959). A well-written and provocative study with lively sections on LeClerc and Bayle. The sections on the English deists and on the Euhemerists and Newton are highly recommended.

McCULLOCH, GERALD O., ed. *Man's Faith and Freedom: The Theological Influence of Jacobus Arminius* (New York: Abingdon Press, 1962). A collection of articles. The most useful are James Luther Adams, "Arminius and the Structure of Society," and

Gerrit Jan Hoenderdaal, "The Life and Struggle of Arminius in the Dutch Republic."

McLACHLAN, H. JOHN. *Socinianism in Seventeenth-Century England* (London: Oxford University Press, 1951). An outstanding book. Chapter III is of great value because of its appreciation of Holland as an intermediary.

MURRAY, JOHN J. *Amsterdam in the Age of Rembrandt* (Norman: University of Oklahoma Press, 1967). A clear, orderly book for students beginning Anglo-Dutch studies.

The Correspondence of Isaac Newton, ed. H. W. Turnbull. 4 Vols. (Cambridge: Cambridge University Press, 1961). Volume III, 1688-1694, offers much first-hand material on Newton's interest in exegesis.

PASSMORE, J. A. *Ralph Cudworth* (Cambridge: Cambridge University Press, 1951). An excellent monograph to be read in conjunction with Rosalie L. Colie's *Light and Enlightenment*.

PIENAAR, W. J. B. *English Influences in Dutch Literature and Justus Van Effen as Intermediary* (Cambridge: Cambridge University Press, 1929). An indispensable work surveying late seventeenth and early eighteenth centuries. Text emphasizes the Dutch contributions.

REESINK, H. J. *L'Angleterre et la Littérature Anglaise dans les Trois plus Anciens Périodiques Français de Hollande de 1684 à 1709* (Paris: Librairie Ancienne Honoré Champion, 1931). A carefully detailed inventory of the Bibliothèques of Bayle, Basnage de Beauval, and LeClerc's BUH. Prefatory essay is a clear description of Dutch and French periodicals.

SANDYS, JOHN EDWIN. *A History of Classical Scholarship.* 3 Vols. (Cambridge: Cambridge University Press, 1908). Still the most complete and readily available account of classical scholarship. Most valuable are the chapters "The Netherlands from 1575 to 1700" and "The Netherlands in the Eighteenth Century."

SELLIN, P. R. *Daniel Heinsius and Stuart England* (London: Oxford University Press, 1968). A much needed work, valuable as a detailed study of a scholar too long neglected.

SHAFTESBURY, ANTHONY, EARL OF. *Characteristics*, ed. John M. Robertson. Vols. I-II. (New York: The Bobbs-Merrill Company, Inc., 1964).

STEPHEN, LESLIE. *History of English Thought in the Eighteenth Century.* 2 Vols. (New York: Harcourt, Brace & World, Inc., 1962). A complete and important work; probably the best study for student use.

STRONG, R. C., AND J. A. VAN DORSTEN. *Leicester's Triumph* (London: Oxford University Press, 1964). A short account, but forms part of the total picture of Anglo-Dutch relations in the late sixteenth century.

TEN HARMSEL, HENRIETTA. *Jacobus Revius* (Detroit: Wayne State University Press, 1968). A collection of Revius's poems, excellently translated. The introduction on this Dutch metaphysical poet is, perhaps, the best critical essay available.

THORNDIKE, LYNN. *A History of Magic and Experimental Science.* 8 Vols. (New York: Columbia University Press, 1958). A standard, reliable work. Volumes VII and VIII deal with the seventeenth century.

VAN DER WELLE, J. A. *Dryden and Holland* (Groningen: J. B. Wolters, 1962). A specialized work which examines Dryden's attitude toward the Dutch and stresses the influence of Dutch philologists.

VAN DORSTEN, JAN ADRIANUS. *Poets, Patrons, and Professors* (Leiden: Universitaire Pers, 1962). A good book for background reading on Anglo-Dutch relationship in Elizabethan England.

VAN DORSTEN, J. A. *Thomas Basson 1555-1613 English Printer at Leiden* (Leiden: Universitaire Pers, 1961). A concentrated study which emphasizes the close ties between England and Leyden.

WEEVERS, THEODOR. *Poetry of the Netherlands in its European Context 1170-1930* (London: The Athlone Press, 1960). An anthology enhanced by a good introduction dealing in general with the history of Dutch poetry.

Index

Aa, Peter Vander, 145
An Abridgement of the Prerogatives of S. Ann . . . , 65
Acta Eruditorum, 32
Addison, Joseph, 33, 41, 42, 59, 70, 91, 92, 95-97, 100, 104, 106, 156, 166n.41; quoted, 36-37
Aesop's Fables, 70, 72
Allix, Pierre, 26, 33, 134
Almoloveen, Theodorus Janssonius ab, 59
Amboyna, 13
Analysis per Quantitatum, Series . . . , 86-87
Aranda, Paul d', 34, 161n.7
Annotations on the New Testament, 28, 43
Arminianism, 20, 30
The Art of Love, 70
The Art of Poetry, 110, 114
Aucti-catalogi, Dutch, 21, 58, 59
Aymon, Jean, 59

Bacon, Francis, 142
Baker, Thomas, quoted, 64, 146-47
Barbeyrac, Jean, 73
Barnes, Annie, 161n.6; quoted, 25
Barnes, Joshua, 17, 42, 58, 69, 71-74
Barrow, Isaac, 64
Basnage de Beauval, Henri, 22, 25, 55, 57-60, 67, 69, 90, 96, 97; quoted, 70
The Battle of the Books, 18, 99
Baudius, Dominicus, 16
Bayle, Pierre, 22, 23, 25, 32, 39, 53, 55-60, 67, 69, 77, 79, 106; quoted, 82
Benoit, Elie, 129
Bentley, Richard, 17, 37, 42, 51-53, 69, 74, 75, 99, 157
Berkeley, George, 70, 85, 87
Bernard, Jacques, 33, 46, 48, 60

Blackmore, Richard, 59, 70
Blount, Thomas Pope, 70
Boendermaker, Theodorus, 59
Boerhaave, Herman, 19, 59, 63
Boileau, Nicholas, 74, 107
Bossuet, Jacques, bishop of Meaux, 69
Bourignon, Antoinette, 129
Boyle, Robert, 19, 39, 59, 64, 69
British attitude toward the Dutch, 14-16, 18-19, 20-21
Broekhuyzen, Jan van, 17, 42, 72-74
Browne, Sir Thomas, 64; quoted, 17
Buchanan, George, 16
Burman, Pieter (the elder), 17, 26, 42, 51-53, 59, 72-74
Burman, Pieter (the younger), 17
Burnet, Gilbert, bishop of Salisbury, 33, 38, 58, 59, 65, 66, 76, 78, 91, 102, 104, 131, 157, 161n.6; quoted, 15, 34, 148
Bury, Arthur, 68

Calamy, Edmund, quoted, 137
The Cambridge University Press, 1696-1712, 40
Camden, William, 17
The Campaign, 97
Casaubon, Isaac, 45, 74, 122, 123
Cats, Jacob, 20, 23
Cave, William, 53, 61, 129, 139-41
Ceno, Charles le, 31
Chamberlayne, John, 46, 48; quoted, 47, 49
Characteristics, 87-90
Charleton, Walter, 64
Chaucer, Geoffrey, 59
The Christian Hero, 59
Clagett, William, 65, 66
Clarendon, Edward Hyde, 3rd Earl of, 70, 93, 94, 116

177